SPIRITUAL ABUNDANCE

*The Quest for
the Presence of God in
Daily Life*

ROBERT L. WISE

A
JANET
THOMA
BOOK

THOMAS NELSON PUBLISHERS
Nashville

Published in Nashville, Tennessee, by Thomas Nelson, Inc. in association with the literary agency of Alive Communications, 7680 Goddard St., Suite 200, Colorado Springs, CO 80920.

Scripture quotations noted NKJV are from THE NEW KING JAMES VERSION. Copyright © 1979, 1980, 1982, 1990 Thomas Nelson, Inc. Scripture quotations noted NASB are from the NEW AMERICAN STANDARD BIBLE®, © Copyright The Lockman Foundation 1960, 1962, 1963, 1968, 1971, 1972, 1973, 1975, 1977. Used by permission. (www.Lockman.org.) Scripture quotations noted NIV are from the HOLY BIBLE: NEW INTERNATIONAL VERSION®. Copyright © 1973, 1978, 1984 by International Bible Society. Used by permission of Zondervan Publishing House. All rights reserved. Scripture quotations noted RSV are from the REVISED STANDARD VERSION of the Bible. Copyright © 1946, 1952, 1971, 1973 by the Division of Christian Education of the National Council of the Churches of Christ in the U.S.A. Used by permission.

Every effort was made to secure permission for all material which may require permission. Anyone with permission information should contact the publisher so that changes can be made in subsequent printings.

"Dear Joanna" (excerpt on p. 58) from *Living by the Word: Selected Writings 1973–1987*, copyright © 1988 by Alice Walker, reprinted by permission of Harcourt, Inc.

Library of Congress Cataloging-in-Publication Data

Wise, Robert L.
    Spiritual abundance : the quest for the presence of God in daily life / Robert L. Wise.
        p. cm.
    Includes bibliographical references.
    ISBN 0-7852-6798-0
        1. Spiritual life—Christianity. I. Title.

BV4501.2.W57413 2001
248.4—dc21   00–046535

Printed in the United States of America
1 2 3 4 5 6 7 8 9 10 BVG 06 05 04 03 02 01

Contents

To
Michael Wise,
number twelve in a wonderful
long line of splendor

PART ONE

* * *

Disconnecting:
The Loss of Soul

ONE

The Journey Begins

Once upon a time I lost my soul.

No horrendous sins or salacious twists. Mephistopheles didn't appear one midnight offering immortality in exchange for my heart's desire. Actually, worthwhile pursuits demanded most of my time.

The busy life of church work, family, being a parent to four children, trying to pay bills without enough money, and intending to do everything well simply took its toll. I lost touch with the center of my being. My soul just disappeared beneath the weight of sacks of groceries, piles of bills, college degrees, and the burden of too many worries and not enough hours in the day for extended prayer, personal reflection, and solace. My spirituality withered from neglect. Strangely, I didn't even notice the loss for a long time. Mistaking busyness for meaning, activity for purpose, the sheer inertia of preoccupation with good things kept me from realizing that I'd lost contact with the best thing. Sixty-hour work weeks have a way of blurring one's vision.

I knew that my spirituality had been slipping. Actually, the word *spirituality* is probably the most used and least understood concept in the English language. We casually use the word to imply getting in touch with God. Spirituality meant that what I couldn't see with my eyes, I would experience in my heart . . . or something of that order. Whatever. Nevertheless, this most important ingredient in my well-being seemed to have slipped away from my life, and I knew that my inner "gas tanks" were approaching empty. More than anything in the world, I needed to find *spiritual abundance.*

DISCOVERING THE ZOMBIES

I remember a growing awareness of being surrounded by multitudes of other people struggling with the same problem of spiritual anemia. I saw their images in nearly every movie I attended (and I saw at least one a week). Anti-heroes had become the new heroes; degenerate people with degrading values gained cinema star status. Gangsters, psychotics, and the promiscuous were Hollywood's fascination. The music industry bestowed on us rappers, Madonna, Mick Jagger, and a host of rock stars (some of whom quickly jettisoned themselves into eternity with drugs) for our adulation. Something was seriously amiss.

Having been in the ministry for many years, I looked to my fellow clergy, brothers and sisters in Christ, to offer me the first clues about my own loss—but I didn't get the help I needed. While many were the finest people in the world, some ministers operated with ambition that would shame a politician. Many professional clergy preached about the problems of the multitudes but were indifferent to the pain of individuals. Others operated the local church with the same spiritual concern that the branch management of Sears used in selling tires. Spirituality was definitely missing. The truth was that most of the clergy I knew were too preoccupied with their own problems to be bothered with mine. I needed something more than what these types had to offer in spiritual vitality.

Many churches attempted to replace spirituality with "something." In the 1960s, the theological enterprise became serious about the business of creating God in our own image. Theologians poured theology into sociological molds. Correct belief was out; nervous activism was in. Much of the subsequent social action did not have even a hint of spiritual reality. At the other end of the spectrum, evangelism often was not helping people recover their spiritual

abundance as much as it was changing their intellectual outlook by creating an emotional moment of
decision "for Jesus." Rather than the emptiness being
filled with the indwelling Christ, the end product was
signing up the starving for church membership. At
the time I didn't understand what I was seeing, but I
recognized the vain and empty terrain, the wasteland
of T.S. Eliot's hollow men. I sensed that I had plenty
of company struggling with the same emptiness.

LOOKING FOR THE
TREASURE IN THE FIELD

My problem first manifested itself as a hunger, an
emptiness, a haunting inner loneliness I couldn't fill
through any relationship. Like so many people, I
really didn't know how to practice the faith I
believed in. I certainly was as straight and correct as
an apostolic shepherd's crook, but the issue was that
I believed in an idea that didn't seem to be doing
anything for me.

One afternoon, I collapsed across my desk,
fatigued. I had worked as hard as I could that day.
With honest faithfulness, I had not broken any great
commandments, but neither had I been filled with
joy and purpose. I was so tired that tears easily filled
my eyes. I'd done as much as I knew how. And now
I was exhausted.

To gain the world and lose one's soul is one thing. Being a good suburban church member and losing your psyche was quite another. I was impoverished and in deep need of respite. More importantly, I recognized that I was another of Eliot's spiritual scarecrows. I needed help.

A quick look back over my college studies revealed that I had spent a great deal of energy studying emotions and how psychotherapy worked. I didn't need more insight into the mind. My learning equipped me to help others struggling with their confusion, but it didn't straighten out my own emptiness. Reading the latest novel or a new book on the latest advances in theology couldn't satisfy where I hurt. I needed instructors who could teach me the meaning of spirituality and help me find a renewed vital relationship with God.

Good things were happening at churches all over town, but I couldn't seem to find anybody who understood the difference that spiritual abundance could make in my life. Most of these people had settled for "getting by" as enough. When I opened my Bible, the Gospels screamed at me that this promise of fullness was really there for me, but I couldn't seem to get my hands around it. And then I accidentally (on God's purpose) stumbled across a Benedictine monastery at Pecos, New Mexico. Of course, I was a Protestant and couldn't see where I would have any place in such a medieval establishment as (of all things) a *monastery*.

Nevertheless, I had heard that the Pecos religious community of men and women devoted themselves to the pursuit of spiritual abundance through study of the Scriptures, contemplation, worship, and the insights of depth psychology. They were eager to share the paths they had found through the detours set up by the modern world. I knew that I needed something silent, isolated, and filled with people who lived the secret of a dynamic Christian life.

After putting my house and family in order, I took a sabbatical, moved into the monastery, and began the rigorous spiritual life, starting every day with community morning prayer at six o'clock. The ensuing weeks proved to be the most valuable of my life and restored the spirituality I needed. During meditation time, I found stepping-stones. Hidden trails appeared in Scripture. I recovered secret spiritual lagoons and cool grottoes of prayer discovered by ancient saints. Each place was a new soul center where spiritual abundance had been hidden.

After six weeks of isolation, study, prayer, and lots of silence, I was ready to come back. The remote mountains around Pecos, New Mexico, had turned out to be filled with new life. On the morning that I drove away from this quaint hideaway, I knew that my candle was lit with a new light. I was going home a new person.

In the following pages, I don't offer you a road map so much as voices, sounds that I heard in my struggle to find spiritual vitality. As I made my pilgrimage, the calls of these saints, friends, and sojourners kept me on track and helped me hear again the sounds of eternity. The excerpts from their writings aren't offered as a quick read but for slow and careful contemplation. Often some of these simple quotes opened doors that I didn't realize had been tightly closed. My prayer is that each page will help you find the same spiritual abundance that has come to mean so much to me.

Finding yourself is not an inward trek like peeling away the sections of an onion until you hit some secret inner essence. Rather, you *are looking for the fingerprint of God in your life.* The task is to follow the direction and advice of those who already know the inner way well and have been touched by Him.

I found that the need is for centering. While pursuing a college art degree, I studied ceramics. Throwing pots on a wheel proved to be one of the most exhilarating experiences of my life. I became so addicted to the wonderful feel of wet clay oozing between my fingers that time would lose all meaning. I was learning that the secret of working the potter's wheel is the same as recovering one's spirituality. Finding the promised abundance requires work.

In *Centering*, Mary Caroline Richards's marvelous

little book on poetry, pottery, and personhood, she wrote:

> As human beings functioning as potters, we center ourselves and our clay. And we all know how necessary it is to be "on center" ourselves if we wish to bring our clay "into center" and not merely to agitate it or bully it. As organisms in the natural rhythms of birth, growth, and death, we experience metamorphosis throughout our lives, as our bodies grow and change from infancy to ripeness, as our capacities for inner experience enlarge and strengthen.[1]

Centering is our all-important clue for where to find the spiritual reality that can invigorate our lives.

The wheel is spinning, and the time has come. Transformation is waiting in the wings. Let's see if we can find our way to the center of your universe . . . and to spiritual abundance.

TWO

Into the Void

$\mathcal{W}$e need to know something is missing before we can go looking for it. Until people realize they have misplaced their spiritual center, religious talk doesn't connect with them on a significant level. To recover the vitality I had lost, I found that it was necessary for me to get in touch with some important dimensions of my life. To begin my search for God's reality in my life, I needed to start with what the loss of spirituality looked like. The displacement of spiritual connectedness takes many shapes and sizes.

On April 20, 1995, the day after the terrorist bombing in Oklahoma City, Joe Davis discovered that his baseball coach was killed in the Alfred P. Murrah Federal Building. On the day of the funeral, Joe's mother brought the twelve-year-old to talk with me. Joe thought I could tell him why someone would blow up a building, killing 168 people, injuring more than 500 people, orphaning 30 children, and leaving 219 others with only one parent.

Everyone who lives through terrible and traumatic times asks Joe's question many times. Why do human beings inflict such pain on each other? Could the loss of spiritual sensitivity offer part of the answer?

Talking with Joe, I became aware of a new aspect of the tragedies filling the history of the twentieth century. We have become accustomed to explaining all deviant behavior in psychological categories: bombers, murderers, thieves, and rapists are labeled psychopaths, sociopaths, psychotics, and character disorder cases. But do any of these diagnoses answer Joe's questions? No. Perhaps contemporary psychology missed the most important category of all: loss of the spiritual essence that makes human beings different from any other creation!

Is it possible that sane people are capable of committing horrible deeds of malice and abuse? Can people lose their perspectives so completely that they hurt others and remain totally indifferent? The answer is painfully obvious. Of course they can. They do that every day of the week.

While loss of spirituality is gradual and a matter of degree, it produces disconnection with God, others, and oneself. Perspective goes askew and consequences are clouded. Actions no longer have meaning. Behavior becomes self-indulgent. Rational people do very irrational things.

Christians *must* be able to make contact with the void in society and speak to the emptiness. Unless Christian people can understand the signs of the illness, their remedy of faith will never be used.

Loss of relationship with God takes many forms: banality . . . materialism . . . duplicity . . . meaninglessness . . . emptiness . . . indifference. In this chapter are readings, clippings, asides that have some of the sounds, conversations, reflections, and indicators of what forfeiture of spiritual connectedness looks like. As I read and thought about these issues, they put me in touch with aspects of my life that had slipped away from me. These readings are a collection of word pictures depicting the crisis that now surrounds millions of Americans. They offer mirrors to help us see ourselves in the light of others' experiences. Consider these examples well. They are the symptoms of a serious disease.

People are incurably religious creatures. Even though we've lost contact with the God of the universe, we have learned how to invent our own religion that doesn't need the real God. Hedonism, entertainment, and banality are the new trinity that masses of people adhere to and believe in. Take a look at the new faith offered through television.

Happiness Is

RUSSELL BAKER

The Gorths have found happiness through faith in television. "Absolute faith in the doctrine of material- ism as revealed on Channels 2, 4, 5, 7, 9, and 20," says Bill, "has made a new person of me."

"Fabulous," says Cora Sue. "Twice as much happi- ness power as my old faith product."

Bill's conversion began one day when, listless, Vietnam- weary and tired of his marriage, he sat in the evening traffic jam slouched at the wheel of his Hupmobile. "Suddenly," he says, "I realized that it wasn't happening. When I got home that night, I told Cora Sue, 'We've got to find something that will make it happen. That night Channel 4 spoke to me for the first time. 'Rhinoceros makes it happen,' Channel 4 said . . .'"

Seeing Bill's new happiness, Cora Sue began taking instructions from Channel 9. One night after Bill had hitched his Rhinoceros at the curb and fought off the beauties swarming to kiss him, he entered the kitchen to find Cora Sue wearing a queen's crown. That afternoon, on the instruction from Channel 9, she had quit greas- ing the bread with the high-priced spread and had switched to new, improved gummoid margarine.

Since that day both Gorths have become contented,

if somewhat hysterical, people. This gives an odd quality to attempts to make conversation with them. Com-
monplace conversational gambits such as, "Why am I
so miserable all the time?" bring answers such as, "It's
that old product you're using on your hair, friend."

"Fabulous," says Cora Sue. "Twice as much anti-
misery power, too."

Like so many converts, the Gorths have no patience
with skeptics. "What! Not believe in the new washday
miracle?" Bill will ask. "Why, man, you might as well
deny the existence of twice as much anti-perspirant
power. You might as well say there is no crunchy goodness flavor packed into every wholesome kernel of
springtime freshness."

Nothing irritates Bill Gorth more than someone
pointing out that he talks like a fool. "Of course I talk
like a fool," he says. "Cora Sue and I both talk like
fools. It is our way of being absolutely loyal to our
belief. Look, this whole neighborhood, this whole city,
this whole country is swarming with people who practice the same faith as we do. The only difference is that
they're ashamed of it. It conceals their shame if they can
laugh at the language of the channels, but it doesn't
stop them from living by the message. Cora Sue and I
believe in being perfectly honest about our faith."

"Fabulous," says Cora Sue. "Twice as much fool-
exposure power, too."

Happiness to Bill and Cora Sue is belief in faster

starting, brighter laundry, quicker relief, fresher smoke, longer protection, shinier floors, crunchier goodness, crisper chips, sexier lips, slimmer hips, and happier trips.

"As a religion," says Bill, "I'll admit it's not much, but at least it is suited to today's world."

"Fabulous," says Cora Sue. "Twice as much fun as that old moralizing, too."

FROM *SOUNDINGS,*
EDITED BY ROBERT A. RAINES, P. 76

———————◆———————

Sound a little "far out"? Every time I read this parody, I chuckle but also know that behind the silliness is the fact that many people have slipped into a mode where entertainment is the "worship experience" that makes their world run spiritually. Who doesn't hear a steady diet of preaching that warns of the seduction of things? Yet, American society has a singular devotion to materialism, the worship of prosperity, status, and the accumulation of things. Without even realizing that it had happened to me, I had allowed such nonsense to blindside me.

Materialism promises that through consumption we can find our way to a meaningful existence. I had to recognize that while I might refute this idea, I was still caught up in much that was promised by contemporary advertising. If I was going to recover my spiritual connectedness, I had to reach out and turn off the tube!

William James once noted that the pursuit of success is our national disease. Once of the reasons that I was tired so often stemmed from my relentless pursuit of standing higher on the social ladder. While our heavenly Father certainly has nothing against our being significant persons, when our pursuit of accomplishment interferes with our relationship with Him, we're in deep trouble. I began to see that I had to make significant adjustments in what I was chasing.

Where do people turn when they've lost their spiritual vitality? Where do they look for warmth and understanding? Consider where people gravitate for a touch of care . . . even if it is artificial.

◆

The Brass Rail Communion Table
GAY TALESE, NOVELIST

It was the sort of West Side bar that even a libel lawyer would call a "dive." The stools were patched, the neon light was cracked, the drinkers seemed tired, dusty and lonely—like the neighborhood. And yet the blonde girl behind the bar did not fit the scene at all. She possessed a just-bathed look and was obviously intelligent and very polite and cheerful. When the other barmaids would steal her tips, she would not complain; when one of the men at the bar would become insulting, she would seem not to hear.

The owner of the bar could never understand why she had applied in June for employment in such a place. He did not know . . . that she was a University of California graduate in sociology, and that the $50 a week summer job behind the bar was part of her "course" in the study of the drinker; the decadent neighborhood, and its effect upon loneliness.

He was not upset, just dumbfounded when Astrid Huerter told him this. And he was astonished too, when she said the employment there had been "very educational." Later Miss Huerter, a twenty-one-year-old native of Germany who got a scholarship to study in this country, said that many of her preconceived notions of life in a dive had proved to be false. There is a kind of "morality" to be found there, she said, and many of the regular drinkers, some of them derelicts, soon began to worry about her, to wonder what "a nice girl like you" is doing in such a place.

"A few of them said they knew of other jobs for me that weren't so low class," she said. "They wanted to rescue me—they who could barely help themselves." Most of the regular patrons, she said, came to the bar not out of a need to drink or to pass the time of night; they came rather "out of a desperate need to communicate with someone and a desire to be heard." If it was merely alcohol that they wanted, they could have got it at half the price from a liquor store; and if they wished merely to pass time, they could have gone to the movies . . . But only in the neighborhood bar could they be certain of being heard and that was her job there—professional listener . . . In New York . . . people do not have time to listen. Here everything is 'getting ahead' and 'progress'—and 'money.' Here you have to pay people to listen. And that is what a barmaid does.

FROM *CREATIVE BROODING*

EDITED BY ROBERT A. RAINES, P. 23

———————◆———————

The first time I read this little description, I was taken aback. I don't spend time in bars and had a rather different impression of what goes on in there in the dark. However, as I read the piece again, I realized that maybe these places filled a function that I had entirely missed. This essay details the idea that a bar is a place where people talk—and maybe try to get in touch with their lost spirituality.

While I certainly wouldn't recommend a bar as a place to go for conversation or counseling, I recognized that part of recovering our spirituality is found through realizing that we do need to communicate with someone who can understand our struggles. We need someone to listen with an accepting heart.

People with open ears and hearts become an important stepping-stone out of the void.

Let's turn our attention and look in another direction. Nothing exposes the *void* like suffering, death, and disillusionment. The personal discovery of duplicity, deceptiveness, and limitation can scatter the facades we live behind . . . and the emptiness they mask. I found that one of the significant "helps" in making me face the doldrums was coming to grips with the contingency and limitedness of my own life. Let me see if I can help get the issue into perspective.

What if you picked up today's paper and discovered your obituary on the funeral page? What would it say? How would you be described? What accomplishments would be listed? And most important, how would it feel to read such a story?

Reading Your Own Obituary
NICHOLAS HALASZ, AUTHOR

One morning in 1888, Alfred Nobel, inventor of dynamite, the man who had spent his life amassing a fortune from the manufacture and sale of weapons of destruction, awoke to read his own obituary. The obituary was printed as a result of a simple journalistic

INTO THE VOID

error—Alfred's brother had died, and a French reporter carelessly reported the death of the wrong brother. Any man would be disturbed under the circumstances, but to Alfred Nobel the shock was overwhelming. He saw himself as the world saw him—"the dynamite king," the great industrialist who had made an immense fortune from explosives. This—as far as the general public was concerned—was the entire purpose of his life. None of his true intentions—to break down the barriers that separated men and ideas—were recognized or given serious consideration. He was quite simply a merchant of death, and for that alone would he be remembered . . . As he read his obituary with horror, Nobel resolved to make clear to the world the true meaning and purpose of his life. This could be done through the final disposition of his fortune. His last will and testament would be the expression of his life's ideals . . . The result was the most valued of prizes given to those who have done most for the cause of world peace.

FROM *CREATIVE BROODING*,
EDITED BY ROBERT A. RAINES, P. 121

If Nobel's life could be so radically changed by considering his own death, what could happen to mine? The thought really haunted me, and I wondered what

19

my friends at the newspaper might write about me and what I had accomplished. I even sat down and started drawing up my own obituary. That little exercise certainly put me in touch with the void in my life!

Sometimes the problem is that we've been hurt and are running from the old pain. No fun there! More than occasionally we simply don't know how to deal with pain and face the struggle that can be so creative even though it hurts. Let me give you a hard example of how difficult life can be and of the pain that can, in turn, wound us so deeply.

You won't have had the experience that Camus describes, but it will give you something to think about.

The Little-Ease and the Spitting Cell

ALBERT CAMUS, AUTHOR

(1913–1960)

Believe me, religions are on the wrong track the moment they moralize and fulminate commandments. God is not needed to create guilt or to punish. Our fellow men suffice, aided by ourselves. You were speaking of the Last Judgment . . . I shall wait for it resolutely, for I have known what is worse, the judgment of men. For them, no extenuating circumstances; even the good intention is ascribed to crime. Have you at least heard of the spitting cell, which a nation recently thought up to prove itself the greatest on earth? A walled-up box in which the prisoner can stand without moving. The solid door that locks him in his cement shell stops at chin level. Hence only his face is visible, and every passing jailer spits copiously on it. The prisoner, wedged into his cell, cannot wipe his face, though he is allowed, it is true, to close his eyes. Well, that, *mon cher,* is a human invention. They didn't need God for that little masterpiece.

What of it? Well, God's sole usefulness would be to guarantee innocence, and I am inclined to see religion rather as a huge laundering venture—as it was once but briefly, for exactly three years and it wasn't called religion. Since then, soap has been lacking, our faces are dirty, and we wipe one another's noses. All dunced, all punished, let's all spit on one another and—hurry! to the little-ease! Each tries to spit first, that's all. I'll tell you a big secret, *mon cher.* Don't wait for the Last Judgment. It takes place every day.

FROM *CREATIVE BROODING,*
EDITED BY ROBERT A. RAINES, P. 51

———◆———

Horrible, huh?
But the point is clear: I may have to wade through

some painful areas of my life to get back to the place where the trouble began.

Let's look in another direction. Chaim Potok's novels have always helped me see new glimpses of how important it is to walk through suffering in order to hear God calling me. *Sometimes the experiences that cut to the quick turn out to be God's special megaphone.* Consider this vignette.

The Silent Father

CHAIM POTOK, AUTHOR

(1929–)

When I was very young, my father, may he rest in peace, began to wake me in the middle of the night, just so I would cry. I was a child, but he would wake me and tell me stories about the destruction of Jerusalem and the sufferings of the people of Israel, and I would cry. For years he did this. Once he took me to visit a hospital—ah, what an experience that was—and often he took me to visit the poor; the beggars, to listen to them talk. My father himself never talked to me, except when we studied together. He taught me with silence. He taught me to look into myself, to find my own strength, to walk around inside myself in company with my soul. When his people would ask him why he was so silent

22

with his son, he would say to them that he did not like to talk, ⌐words are cruel, words play tricks, they distort what is in the heart, they conceal the heart, the heart speaks through silence. ⌐One learns of the pain of others by suffering one's own pain, he would say, by turning inside oneself, by finding one's own soul. And it is important to know of pain, he said. It destroys our self-pride, our arrogance, our indifference toward others. It makes us aware of how frail and tiny we are and of how much we must depend upon the Master of the universe.⌐ Only slowly, very slowly, did I begin to understand what he was saying. For years his silence bewildered and frightened me, though I always trusted him, I never hated him. And when I was old enough to understand, he told me that of all people, a tzaddik [a spiritual leader by example, or a righteous person] especially must know of pain. A tzaddik must know how to suffer for his people, he said. He must take their pain from them and carry it on his own shoulders. He must cry, in his heart he must always cry. Even when he dances and sings, he must cry for the sufferings of his people.

FROM *SOUNDINGS*,
EDITED BY ROBERT A. RAINES, P. 80

———————◆———————

And what does the *tzaddik* receive for facing up to this hard task of suffering with and for his people?

One thing is for sure: He doesn't live with a spiritual void in his life.

I don't want to live with the results of bombings, loneliness, pain, illness, and nonsense, but if I have to reside there in order to become spiritually alive, then I will. I know that the journey to spiritual abundance is more than worth the struggle.

Think about it. Maybe this is where *you* have to begin.

THREE

The Loneliness

One of the hallmarks of our time has been the quest for a "religionless age," a society without God, an explanation of the meaning of life without faith. Movies are made and plays are written as if God doesn't even exist. And what does such a world look like, smell like, taste like? As we enter the twenty-first century, we now know. The singular word describing the consequence is—*empty*.

Christians often forget what it is to swim in such an existence without a lifeline or reprieve. The better we understand the emptiness, the more adept we are at articulating the answer—*lost*.

One evening I looked out of the church office and saw a forlorn figure shuffling across the parking lot. Pastors, ministers, and priests become accustomed to panhandlers slithering in, looking for an easy touch. Even when we know they are conning us, we clergy still struggle to find the right words.

But this man looked different.

The tattered figure was thin, the face gaunt. His feet barely cleared the pavement as he tottered forward. His eyes were empty and his mouth slightly open. He kept grimacing and shaking.

I listened more carefully than usual as the tall, skinny man tried to tell me what he wanted. He said his name was Jack, and his landlord was going to evict him. Jack was fifty and had no idea where to go or what to do. He wasn't desperate so much as hopeless. I quickly concluded that he was clinically depressed and on the verge of suicide.

Jack's vacant stare became a mirror, and I took a second look at myself. There, but for the grace of God, went I . . .

Often we don't know what is right until everything has gone wrong. In the emptiness, we remember what fullness meant.

A year earlier, Jack's wife had died. With no children and the rest of his family gone, Mary was all he had in the whole world. When she died, his will to work, to play, to do anything evaporated. Thirty days later the company fired him, and Jack hadn't worked since. The center of his existence had crumbled. His soul died.

Different individuals experience loss in different

ways. Listening to their discoveries brings us to our own awareness of what might be missing in our own lives. Let's take another look at what the loss of a soul is like. Listen to some hollow voices, lonely sounds, and see if the emptiness reminds you of something missing in yourself. Voices can whistle down lonely streets like the winter wind on a cold, forlorn night, sending coldness racing through us. Here are some of the sounds of silence, the moans of failure, and the signs of loneliness as they arise from the conclusions of people who have lost the center of life. Anything sound familiar to you?

Hollywood's a place where they'll pay you a thousand dollars for a kiss and fifty cents for your soul.

—MARILYN MONROE

Truly one learns only by sorrow; it is a terrible education the soul gets, and it requires a terrible grief that shakes the very foundation of one's being to bring the soul into its own.

—BRITISH MAJOR LANOE GEORGE HAWKER

Soul loss can be observed today as a psychological phenomenon in the everyday lives of the human beings around us. Loss of soul appears in the form of a sudden onset of apathy and listlessness; the joy has gone out of life, initiative is crippled, one feels empty, everything seems pointless.

—MARIE-LOUISE VON FRANZ

Loneliness is the anxiety that you do not matter at all.

—JOYCE HUGGETT

Loneliness is an unhappy compound of having lost one's point of reference, of suffering the fate of individual and collective discontinuity, and of living through or dying from a crisis of identity to the point of alienation of one's self.

—DR. LUDWIG BINSWANGER

Life is a dead-end street.

—H. L. MENCKEN

———————◆———————

These folks make life sound tough, don't they? But haven't you had many of these thoughts yourself? Sure. We all do. Somewhere between the innocence of childhood and the despair of old age, disillusionment settles over many people like an emotional Alzheimer's disease. Joy gives way to cynicism, and despondency reigns. Periodically I have to stop and get in touch with the truth about where I am on my life's journey. Pessimism can slip under my skin and make me cynical before I realize the symptoms of what's occurred. I find that I must stop and think about why these voices resonate with me. I have to dig into what's gone wrong inside my life. Listen some more.

Life is a wonderful thing to talk about, or to read about in history books—but it is terrible when one has to live it.

—JEAN ANOUILH

Life is a disease; and the only difference between one man and another is the stage of the disease at which he lives.

—GEORGE BERNARD SHAW

Life is a zoo in a jungle.

—PETER DE VRIES

Pity is for the living; envy is for the dead.

—MARK TWAIN

I am leaving because I am bored.

—GEORGE SANDERS, IN HIS SUICIDE NOTE

To me, death is not a fearful thing. It's living that's cursed.

—Jim Jones, Jonestown, Guyana, 18 November 1978

I just have this feeling that our generation is dying away. There's Kurt [Cobain] and River Phoenix. The aimless quality of my age. The job situation. I think a lot of people think they're not understood, that their parents don't understand them, that society has no place for them because of their age.

—Johanna Pirko, age 18

In a real dark night of the soul, it is always three o'clock in the morning.

—F. Scott Fitzgerald

To live is the rarest thing in the world. Most people exist, that is all.

—Oscar Wilde

We are always getting ready to live, but never living.

—Ralph Waldo Emerson

The peculiar malaise of our day is air-conditioned unhappiness, the staleness and stuffiness of machine-made routine.

—Rabbi Eugene Borowitz

There is nothing more tragic than to find an individual bogged down in the length of life, devoid of breadth.

—MARTIN LUTHER KING JR.

It is my conviction that a very large part of mankind's ills and of the world's misery is due to the rampant practice of trying to feed the soul with the body's food.

—FRANK FARRELL

I live day to day, and life is a constant struggle that we win and lose on a daily basis.

—CHER

Papillon, the French prisoner who was condemned to life imprisonment on Devil's Island, suffered from a recurring nightmare. Each night he would dream that he stood in judgment before a merciless tribunal. "You are charged," the words echoed, "with a wasted life. How do you plead?" In his dream he knelt in abject guilt and replied, "Guilty, I plead guilty."

—UNKNOWN

◆

I have found that two doors open in front of meaninglessness and despair. One is marked "Nowhere" and the other "Promise." The first leads to oblivion, the other to recovery. The lonely must have the courage to persevere. If you've found that the previous quotes touch a sensitive place, then you've found an important clue about where you need to look next. Emptiness may be the prelude to a new symphony of fullness in your life.

In 1978, Alexander Solzhenitsyn warned America: "We have placed too much hope in political and social reforms, only to find out that we were being deprived of our most precious possession: our spiritual life."[1] The Russian writer understood how important spiritual vitality is to our sense of well-being. Current surveys and trends reveal a new intensity in the search for spiritual meaning across this land. Possibly, Americans have "hit bottom" and concluded, in their helplessness, that they need the spiritual vitality that only God can impart. Some years ago the well-known pastor and preacher Chuck Swindoll made an important observation. He said, "We have become a generation of people who worship our work, who work at our play, and who play at our worship." Maybe the time has come for you to stop trying to worship in your office and start working at worshiping in a church.

FOUR

Soul Eaters:
Spiritual Cannibalism

*W*hat does it look like when spiritual Draculas invade our town and lurk about on dark street corners? Not like the images of the old Bela Lugosi flicks of the 1930s. Instead, the pictures come pouring into our living rooms every night. Some estimates say children will see more than 26,000 murders and other acts of violence on television before they graduate from high school. The result is a growing trivialization of suffering and human pain, along with an increasing acceptance of brutal violence as normal. We are surrounded by a culture of death.

Is such a shift anything other than a massive death of soul?

The time is long overdue to face the toll we pay for spiritual cannibalism.

We have gained freedom without responsibility, prosperity without values, and affluence without spirituality. Our voyage through the twentieth century has taken us to many ports of no return. Never has it been more clear that it is possible to gain the world and lose our souls!

Here's what the entertainment industry has to offer us.

Are Music and Movies Killing America's Soul?

RICHARD LACAYO, WRITER

Over at Taco Bell, 15-year-old Christopher Zahedi will tell you he prefers the rougher stuff. "I liked the part in *Pulp Fiction* where the guy points a gun and says a prayer from the Bible and then kills everybody," he offers. "You hear the gun go brrr. It's cool. . . ."

The complications set in during the '90s, when the boomers who were once pop culture's most dedicated consumers became the decision makers at media companies—but also the parents of the next generation. Pulled one way by their lifelong instinct for whatever is sensational, unsanitized, or unofficial, they find themselves dragged in the other direction by their emerging second thoughts as citizens and parents.

In the aftermath of the Oklahoma City bombing, the conservatives are also struck with their own problem of violence in the media—and it's not just Schwarzenegger's body counts. "Jackbooted thugs," the description of federal law-enforcement agents in a fund-raising letter from the National Rifle Association, is a kind of cop-killer lyric in itself. So is "aim at the head" radio talk-show host G. Gordon Liddy's suggestion for getting federal law-enforcement agents at your door.[1]

TIME, 12 JUNE 1995, PP. 24–30

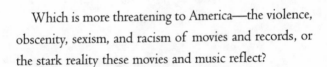

Which is more threatening to America—the violence, obscenity, sexism, and racism of movies and records, or the stark reality these movies and music reflect?

—JOHN EDGAR WIDEMAN, AUTHOR AND PROFESSOR

Yes, the entertainment industry is an empty, soulless empire. I can't bring myself to defend many of the films now made . . . Hollywood must examine itself. Its greed is sickening. It must judge the social impact, not just the popularity impact, of what it does. So must politicians who seek to exploit cultural values.

—PAUL SCHRADER, SCREENWRITER AND DIRECTOR

I, too, dislike many pop-culture products, although probably not the ones that bother Senator [Robert] Dole.

But, the fact is, no system of regulation or voluntary restraint is going to have much effect on mass entertainment. And I'd like to hear how Dole squares his antiviolence stand with his ardent support for the N.R.A. and the overturning of the assault-weapons ban. Guns don't kill people; rap music kills people? Oliver Stone movies kill people? Please.

—KATHA POLLITT, POET, WRITER, AND SOCIAL CRITIC

Sadly, the U. S. has become the land of easy sex and uneasy souls.

—BETSY ROSS, NEW YORK CITY CITIZEN,
FROM *TIME-FORUM*, 12 JUNE 1995, P. 3

———◆———

America, What's Gone Wrong?
WILLIAM J. BENNETT, AUTHOR

The world still regards the United States as the leader in economic and military power, but no longer as the moral leader we once were.

Many foreigners come here believing they are visiting a degraded society, but violence and urban terror are only part of the picture. The ultimate insult from one immigrant student to another is, "You're becoming American." Foreign students are often more diligent and motivated than their American counterparts.

In the industrialized world, America ranks near the top in abortions, divorces, unwed births, and murder, but near the bottom in elementary and secondary school achievement scores. Other factors, not so easily seen or measured, also indicate decline. Morally, a coarseness, cynicism, and vulgarity now characterize our society. Yet our biggest problem is that we're not angry enough about these issues. We have become too accustomed to the cultural rot around us.

Many wish to blame liberal politicians, material-ism, or consumerism for our decline. The real source, however, is an indifference, even an aversion, to spiri-tual matters. The effort to remove God from public life continues, and even privately, people are turning away from God. Historically, when millions of people stop believing in God, enormous public consequences follow.

Americans have put too much hope in politics as the solution to our problems. Politics can never cure moral and spiritual ills. In public policy, we say one thing and do another: for example, we say we want law and order, yet allow violent criminals to return to the streets.

Until 25 years ago, the universally recognized goal of education was the moral and intellectual training of the young. We must return to that belief. We must return religion to its rightful place, both in individual lives and in society. We must refuse to accept the end of moral man; we must carry on the fight, pushing back against the evil forces that push hard against us, so we can save our children from the decadence of our time.[2]

FROM *CURRENT THOUGHTS AND TRENDS*,
JULY 1994, P. 24

———————◆———————

A Nation's Spiritual Decay
WILLIAM J. BENNETT, AUTHOR

The Long Island Rail Road massacre in early December [1993] temporarily shook Americans. But the fact that it took a shower of bullets and a blood-splattered suburban railway car to get our attention speaks volumes about our complacency toward the crime and violence tearing our society apart.

Unfortunately, there are plenty of examples. A New York jury recently awarded a criminal $4.3 million. As he was fleeing the scene after a violent robbery attack that almost killed a 72-year-old man, a transit cop shot him in the back, paralyzing him. The thug won millions for his "pain and suffering"; the elderly man won a trip to the hospital. The public reaction was virtual silence.

During last year's Los Angeles riots, a news camera filmed Damian Williams and Henry Watson pulling an innocent man out of his truck, crushing his skull with a brick, and doing a victory dance over his fallen body.

The lawyers of the young men obtained acquittals on most counts by building a legal defense on the proposition that individuals cannot be held accountable for getting caught up in mob violence. Much of the public wasn't irate, it was relieved.

These outward manifestations—and our complacency about them—are signs of a deeper decay. There is a coarseness, a callousness, a cynicism, a banality and a vulgarity to our time. There are too many signs of a civilization gone rotten. The worst of it has to do with our children.

We live in a culture that at times almost seems dedicated to the corruption of the young, to ensuring the loss of their innocence before their time.

Pop culture plays a key role in this devaluing of America. An indicted murder suspect, Snoop Doggy Dog, recently saw his rap album *Doggystyle* debut at number 1 on the charts. On the daytime television talk shows, indecent exposure is celebrated as a virtue. In recent weeks, these shows have dealt with: cross-dressing couples; a three-way love affair; a man whose chief aim in life is to sleep with women and fool them into thinking he is using a condom; women who can't say no to cheating; prostitutes who love their jobs; and an interview with a young girl caught in the middle of a bitter custody battle.

The real crisis of our time is spiritual. The ancients called it *acedia*—spiritual sloth or deadening, an undue concern for external affairs and worldly things and an absence of zeal for divine things. It eventually leads to a hatred of good altogether.

When millions of people stop believing in God, or when their belief is so attenuated as to be belief in name only, enormous public consequences follow. We can achieve full employment and dynamic economic growth—we can build cities of gold and alabaster— but if our children have not learned to walk in goodness, justice and mercy, then the American experiment, no matter how gilded, will have failed.

Only when we turn our affections and desires toward the right things—toward enduring, noble, spiritual things—will our problems get better . . .

Sadly, in America today the only respectable form of bigotry remaining is bigotry against religious people. If the ancients had a respect for the role religion plays in life, the moderns of our time hate religion because it forces them to confront matters they would prefer to ignore.

But we ignore them at our peril. It now requires a madman's sick episode of violence to touch us at our core. It is to that core we must attend.

FROM *THE SOWER*, SPRING 1994, P. 10

A Jewish Conservative Looks at Pagan America

DON FEDER, AUTHOR

When a rap song that calls for the murder of cops climbs to the top of the charts; when taxpayers are told that their objections to subsidizing a photograph of one man urinating into the mouth of another constitute censorship (when critics consecrate the same as the highest expression of the aesthetic); when a state's voters come within a hair's breadth of legalizing medical murder in the name of relieving suffering; when a presidential candidate informs voters that whether or not he violated his marriage vows is none of their business, we may as well declare intellectual bankruptcy and have the nation placed in moral receivership.

FROM *DISCIPLESHIP JOURNAL*, SEPTEMBER/OCTOBER 1993, P.16

America has a serious problem when $25 can buy a gun and end a life.

—ADAM BITNER, BARRINGTON, W. VA. CITIZEN, FROM "LETTERS TO THE EDITOR," *TIME*, 23 AUGUST 1993

41

———————◆———————

Bang! You're Dead, America

YOUTHWORKER UPDATE, NOVEMBER 1994

In 1991 alone, bullets deprived Americans of 1.1 million years of potential life. Fatalities from gunshot wounds are the fourth leading cause of premature death. Only injuries, cancer, and heart disease take more lives. (The Centers for Disease Control and Prevention arrived at the 1.1 million figure by subtracting the age of gunshot victims from a life expectancy of 65 years.)

The fact that [my] column has been a success underscores, for me at least, the central tragedy of our society, the disconnectedness, the insecurity, the fear that bedevils, cripples, and paralyzes so many of us. I have learned that financial success, academic achievement, and social or political status open no doors to peace of mind or inner security. We are all wanderers, like sheep, on this planet . . .

Suicide is the second most frequent cause of death among teenagers in this country. (The first is accidents.) Every 90 minutes a teenager in America will kill himself. I am firmly against censorship, but where is the moral outrage against all the filth? It's almost impossible to find a family movie these days. What has happened to plain, everyday decency?

FROM *CURRENT THOUGHTS AND TRENDS*, JANUARY 1995, P. 33

We Must Learn Why We Are Producing Such Violent People

WILLIAM RASPBERRY, NEWSPAPER COLUMNIST

I don't want to convict the two eighteen-year-olds charged in the death of Michael Jordan's father. It'll be a while before we know whether the prosecutors can make the case they've been laying out to reporters.

But we already know enough about the two suspects, Larry Demery and Daniel Green, to wonder where such kids come from—and how we can stop producing more of them. And—please—let's not chalk it up to poverty.

Where do these kids come from? The judicial system, bad schools, inadequate parenting and, of course, poverty will get their share of the blame. But there is something more.

There is a generational, ethical and cultural divide that keeps some of us from understanding the rest of us. Some of us (still the majority?) cannot imagine shooting anyone else except to protect our own life or that of a loved one—not for a million dollars, let alone for the short-term thrill of driving a Lexus. We cannot imagine smashing a cinder block over some woman's head in order to make off with seven dollars and a pocketful of cheap jewelry. We cannot imagine gunning down rivals, except in self-defense, and certainly we cannot imagine killing strangers because they have something we want.

And yet there are growing numbers of youngsters who will kill for leather jackets or a pair of sneakers.

If we are to save ourselves, we will have to learn to turn off the spigot that keeps spewing new violence-prone youngsters. We've got to teach them early, as we were taught, the values that make civilized society possible, and we've got to show them that our values work.

Locking up those whose violence mocks our attitudes and beliefs may be necessary but it's not enough. We've got to re-create ourselves.

FROM *THE DALLAS MORNING NEWS*,
23 AUGUST 1993, P. 13A

◆

Most people sell their souls and live with a good conscience on the proceeds.

—LOGAN PEARSALL SMITH

Sin is whatever obscures the soul.

—ANDRÉ GIDE

If you are losing your leisure, look out; you may be losing your soul.

—LOGAN PEARSALL SMITH

44

The tragedy of life is what dies inside a man while he lives.

—ALBERT EINSTEIN

✗ The danger is not lest the soul should doubt whether there is any bread, but lest, by a lie, it should persuade itself that it is not hungry.

—SIMONE WEIL

———————◆———————

What are some conclusions we might draw in the face of such overwhelming evidence that we live in an age of spiritual cannibalism? One clear deduction is that we are surrounded by experiences (often called entertainment) that eat away at our spiritual vitality. A person cannot maintain an intimate relationship with God and be constantly sucked into the depths of a culture of death. We have to make decisions and step out of the muck and mire. If we wait too long, we will drown in the depths of degradation.

The issues of violence, sexism, racism, and the constant depiction of murder and mayhem are not verbal debates between people of different perspectives. In fact, they are matters that will devour all of our spiritual energy. I'm not talking about being a prude or puritanical. The issue is what has always and forever eaten away at the human soul and devoured spirituality. If we wish to have the voice of God ringing through our thoughts, then we must cut off the outside forces that will kill all possibilities of closeness with our heavenly Father.

The moment is at hand. Are we willing to pay the small price of flipping the television switch or not going to a destructive movie? Dare we stand against those forces that are promoting the hurricane conditions that are devouring so many of our youth?

Dare we not?

FIVE

The Contemporary Hunger

*A*bove the empty noise of the clogged streets of modern megalopolis, voices can still be heard crying out for what has been lost. The poets, writers, artists, and people with spiritual vitality in this impersonal age know there is more to life than what they can see around them. Such searchers will not settle for the emptiness of the multitudes struggling off to the grave without assurance they were ever really alive.

An anthology of this quest helps us get a feel of where many people are today as they seek to find spiritual reality. These assembled works better enable us to get in touch with our own center (or its absence). Musing through such writings also enables us to ask more precisely about where the inner places are from which our spiritual strength might arise.

From the past several centuries, these chasers after God and personhood tell us about the haunts visited in their desperate search for meaning. Some ask the question in religious language, and others are thoroughly secular. Either way, they are scouting the same terrain we're searching.

Let's listen for the cries in the night, the moans of pain over lost love and destroyed destiny, as well as the aahs and oohs when discovery has been rich. These humans have not yet given up on humanity. Sometimes they speak of the soul; other times they write of spirituality. Either way, they are essentially after the same thing. Listening to them will hopefully help us in our quest for spiritual vitality.

Streams in the Soul

RUDOLF STEINER,
GERMAN ANTHROPOSOPHIST
(1861–1925)

Anyone who looks deeply into the life of the soul will see that these two streams, one from the past and one from the future, are continually meeting there. The fact that we are influenced by the past is obvious: Who could deny that our energy or idleness of yesterday has some effect on us today? But we ought not to deny the reality of the future, either; for we can observe in the soul the intrusion of future events, although they have not yet happened. After all, there is such a thing as fear of something likely to happen tomorrow, or anxiety about it. Is that not a sort of feeling or perception concerned with the future? Whenever the soul experiences fear or anxiety, it shows by the reality of its feelings that it is reckoning not only with the past but in a very lively manner with something hastening towards it from the future. These, of course, are single examples, but they will find numerous others to contradict the abstract logic which says that since the future does not yet exist, it can have no present influence.

Thus there are these two streams, one from the past and one from the future, which come together in the soul (will anyone who observes himself deny that?) and produce a kind of whirlpool, comparable to the confluence of two rivers . . . Is there anything that can give the soul a sense of security in this situation? Yes, there is. It is what we may call a feeling of humbleness towards anything that may come towards the soul out of the darkness of the future. But this feeling will be effective only if it has the character of prayer. Let us avoid misunderstanding. We are not extolling something that might be called humbleness in one sense or another; we are describing a definite form of it—humbleness to whatever the future may bring. Anyone who looks anxiously and fearfully toward the future hinders his development, hampers the free unfolding to his soul-forces. Nothing, indeed, obstructs this development more than fear and anxiety in face of the unknown future. But the results of submitting to the future can be judged only by experience. What does this humbleness mean?

Ideally, it would mean saying to oneself: Whatever the next hour or day may bring, I cannot change it by fear or anxiety, for it is not yet known. I will therefore wait for it with complete inward restfulness, perfect tranquility of mind. Anyone who can meet the future in this calm, relaxed way, without impairing his active strength and energy, will be able to develop the powers of his soul freely and intensively.

METAMORPHOSES OF THE SOUL, VOL. 2, PP. 43–45

A Child's Question

When I wake up early, and our dog really wants to go out, and he leaps on my bed, and I know he won't let me go back to sleep, I just know it—he'll lick my face, and he'll whine, and he'll lean against me hard, real hard—and when I give up and take him out, and I just stand there, and it's still dark, and you can hear your dog sniffing, it's that quiet: It's then I know there's someone up there, maybe God, maybe lots of people, too, the souls of all the dead folks. It's too big for you to figure out. My dad tells me that when I ask him about God and where heaven is and if there's a soul. He says there is definitely a soul, but it's not "physical," so I shouldn't keep asking him, "Where is it?"

He's right; you can ask too many questions! That's me—always trying to find out answers to everything! I wish you could find them [souls]. In the last year or so, I've sort of slowed down asking! I just look up there and say, "Maybe!" I was walking our dog in the park—there are souls out there, and they must want to talk with someone. I guess they talk with each other. But how? Where are they? Dad says he thinks when you die, your soul dies with you. But then, it's not a soul, it's your mind he's talking about, isn't it? It's probably best just to forget everything except what you have to do today, and the same thing with tomorrow. The only thing is, when you go to Hebrew school and *schul* [synagogue], they tell you God is with us, the Jews, and your soul is His gift to you, that's what the rabbi told us kids when he visited our classroom, and I was going to ask him where in your body God puts the soul He gives you, but I decided that I'd be getting myself into real trouble, because the Hebrew school teacher says I ask too many questions, and I should learn Hebrew and read from Torah and stop trying to be a "philosopher king." Well, what's that? Yes, I asked. The teacher didn't think it was funny, my question. He said, "No more questions!" If I'd raised my hand like that, when the rabbi came to visit our class, I think the teacher would have taken that [blackboard] point of his and charged me with it, like in

the Middle Ages, when the knights went after each other
with swords or spears.[1]

FROM *THE SPIRITUAL LIFE OF CHILDREN* BY ROBERT COLES

Tenderness, Soul, and Saint Teresa
RAYMOND CARVER, AMERICAN AUTHOR
(1939–1988)

Saint Teresa, that extraordinary woman who lived
373 years ago, said: "Words lead to deeds . . . They prepare the soul, make it ready, and move it to tenderness."

There is clarity and beauty in that thought expressed
in just this way. I'll say it again, because there is also
something a little foreign in this sentiment coming to
our attention at this remove, in a time certainly less
openly supportive of the important connection
between what we say and what we do: "Words lead to
deeds . . . They prepare the soul, make it ready, and
move it to tenderness."

Tenderness—that's another word we don't hear much
these days and certainly not on such a public, joyful
occasion as this. Think about it: when was the last time
you used the word or heard it used? It's in a short sup-
ply as that other word, *soul.*

There is a wonderfully described character named
Moiseika in Chekhov's story "Ward No. 6" who, although

he has been consigned to the madhouse wing of the hospital, has picked up the habit of a certain kind of tenderness. Chekhov writes: "Moiseika likes to make himself useful. He gives his companions water, and covers them up when they are asleep; he promises each of them to bring him back a kopeck, and to make him a new cap; he feeds with a spoon his neighbor on the left, who is paralysed."

Even though the word *tenderness* isn't used, we feel its presence in these details, even when Chekhov goes on to enter a disclaimer by way of this commentary on Moiseika's behavior: "He acts in this way, not from compassion nor from any considerations of a humane kind, but through imitation, unconsciously dominated by Gromon, his neighbor on the right hand."

In a provocative alchemy, Chekhov combines words and deeds to cause us to reconsider the origin and nature of tenderness. Where does it come from? As a deed, does it still move the heart, even when abstracted from humane motives?

Somehow, the image of the isolated man performing gentle acts without expectation or even self-knowledge stays before us as an odd beauty we have been brought to witness. It may even reflect back upon our own lives with a questioning gaze.

There is another scene from "Ward No. 6" in which two characters, a disaffected doctor and an imperious postmaster, his elder, suddenly find themselves discussing the human soul.

"And you do not believe in the immortality of the soul?" the postmaster asks suddenly.

"No, honoured Mihail Averyanitch; I do not believe it, and have no grounds for believing it."

"I must own I doubt it, too," Mihail Averyanitch admits. "And yet I have a feeling as though I should never die. Oh, I think to myself, 'Old fogey, it is time you were dead!' But there is a little voice in my soul that says: 'Don't believe it; you won't die.'"

The scene ends but the words linger as deeds. "A little voice in the soul" is born. Also the way we have perhaps dismissed certain concepts about life, about death, suddenly gives over unexpectedly to belief of an admittedly fragile but insistent nature.

Long after what I've said has passed from your minds, whether it be weeks or months, and all that remains is the sensation of having attended a public occasion, marking the end of one significant period of your lives and the beginning of another; try then, as you work out your individual destinies, to remember that words, the right true words, can have the power of deeds.

Remember, too, that little-used word that has just about dropped out of public and private usage: *tenderness.* It can't hurt. And that other word: *soul*—call it spirit if you want, if it makes it any easier to claim the territory.

FROM *NO HEROICS, PLEASE*

As the streams from the past and the future flow together within me, do they produce a tenderness? A compassion for those around me? Do I find that tenderness naturally rises up within me? To be honest, I would have to say that it's been my experience that the longer most people live, the more that tendency is likely to diminish.

The quality is so rare that I find people around me are hungry to see deeds of simple compassion. I would have to conclude that the recovery of spirituality should produce a natural inclination toward kindness and tenderness. I think that a part of what drew people toward Saint Teresa was the sense that such warmth worked in and through her.

Consider another story pointing toward the same inner sensitivity.

The Legend of St. Elmo's Fire

FROM THE JOURNAL OF EDOUARD CORBIERE,

A NINETEENTH-CENTURY SAILOR

During a stormy night one noticed on board fires that played at each end of our main yard. This bright and blue flame, like those that one lights on a punch that is served in cafes, aroused my curiosity for the first time.

"What on earth is that?" I asked a sailor in amazement.

"Saint Elmo's fire, sir."

"Ah, yes, it burns!"

"One had better say that is the sailor's friend. Do you see that kind of flame? Well, if the officer of the watch told me 'Climb up by yourself, pull down the small top-sail' [which is in fact quite heavy for just one man], I would pull it down on the double because that fire would go with me up the rigging to help me, as it helps all sailors."

"But how can you take such a story seriously? It is quite simply, as I remember having read, a natural effect, an electrical discharge that, like a fluid of this kind, seeks points."

"How can I believe that story? An effect of lubricity, electrical discharge, as you please. But it is no less true that that fire, which resembles a glass of brandy that is alight, is the soul of a poor sailor who drowned in the sea in a storm. So you see, when the weather is about to get worse, the soul of the sailors who have taken one drink too many from the great pond, comes and warns their comrades that a dangerous storm is approaching."

"My word, just in case it is true, I want to see if I can touch the soul of a dead man, and I shall go straight to the running board of the yardarm to catch up with your Saint Elmo's fire."

I climbed to the end of the yardarm, as I had said I would, to the great surprise of my companion, who saw a kind of profanation in the intention that I had of going needlessly to bother what he called the sailor's friend.

As my hand gradually got closer to the Saint Elmo's fire, the fluid moved up and down and away and did not come back until I had withdrawn it. This sort of little war between it and myself greatly amused the men of the watch, and they said to me again and again:

"Oh, that one is meaner than you or us."

A sailor from the Lower Brittany cried out to me: "Do you want me to make it disappear?"

"Yes," I replied.

And he made the sign of the cross. The fire did indeed vanish at that very moment . . .

FROM *THE SLAVE TRADER*, PP. 43–45

What do you think about a story like this one? I find that many people I know hunger for such stories to be true. Like the television show *Touched by an Angel*, they hope that in some tangible way the hand of God is working on and around them. They want to believe that maybe Roma Downey will show up on their porch and turn out to be a genuine angel sent to them. Our contemporary lack of spiritual abundance only intensifies our yearning for divine intervention. Since many of us don't have any idea about where we can find God, we settle for the sound-effects or the stage setting left over from His last reported sighting.

Look in another direction and see what you can learn from the emotional experience of African Americans.

Dear Joanna

ALICE WALKER, AFRICAN-AMERICAN AUTHOR

Sometime during the early seventies I was asked to write a letter to an imaginary young black woman, giving her some sense of my own experiences and telling her things she might need to know. I wrote a long letter, which I sent off to the person who asked for it (I no longer recall who this was), but then discovered I wanted to say even more.

Dear Joanna:

Forgive me for writing again so soon. I realize you are busy reading the words of all your other sisters who also love you, but you have been constantly on my mind each day. I think of new things to share with you. Today I wanted to tell you about beauty.

In you, there is beauty like a rock.

So distilled, so unshatterable, so ageless, it will

attract great numbers of people who will attempt, almost as an exercise of will (and of no more importance to them than an exercise), to break it. They will try ignoring you, flattering you, joining you, buying you, simply to afford themselves the opportunity of finding the one crack in your stone of beauty by which they may enter with their tools of destruction. Often you will be astonished that, while they pursue their single-minded effort to do this, they do not seem to see your sorrowing face (sorrowing because some of them will have come to you in the disguise of friends, even sisters) or note the quavering of your voice, or the tears of vulnerability in your eyes. To such people, your color, your sex, your self make you an object. But an object, strangely, perversely, with a soul. A soul.

It is your soul they want.

They will want to crack it out of the rock and wear it somewhere—not inside them, where it might do them good, but about them—like, for example, a feather through their hair, or a scalp dangling from their belt.

As frightening as this is, it has always been so.

Your mother and father, your grandparents, their parents, all have had your same beauty like a rock, and all have been pursued, often hunted down like animals, because of it. Perhaps some grew tired of resisting, and in weariness relinquished the stone that was their life. But most resisted to the end. The end, for them, being merely you. Your life. Which is not an end.

That resistance is your legacy.

Inner beauty, an irrepressible music, certainly courage to say No or Yes, dedication to one's own God, affection for one's own spirit, a simplicity of approach to life, will survive all of us through your will.

You are, perhaps, the last unconquered resident on this earth. And must live, in any case, as if it must be so.

FROM *LIVING BY THE WORD: SELECTED WRITINGS*, PP. 75–78

I've always liked Alice Walker's work, but she especially touched me with this piece. She's right; there are people out there who want your soul. It doesn't make any difference if you're black, white, red, or green. A certain type of person has a morbid curiosity about what's inside other people. They want to pull it out, toy with it for a while, and then discard your essence as if it had no meaning. They simply drop you and your spirituality in a trash can like a used candy wrapper.

Why are they like this? I believe their behavior is

another form of depraved spiritual hunger. Having lost their own spirituality, they no longer realize how extremely important *that same spirituality* is to another person. Like fools watching dogs fight, they walk away without realizing that their own lives are hanging in the balance.

In contrast, let me offer you a little relief. Sheila Ferguson cooked up a little something for you. Take a bite.

Soul Food

SHEILA FERGUSON,
AFRICAN-AMERICAN SINGER AND AUTHOR

Ah, soul food. Soul is just what the name implies. It is soulfully cooked food or richly flavored foods good for your ever-loving soul. But soul food is much more than a clever name penned by some unknown author. It is a legacy clearly steeped in tradition; a way of life that has been handed down from generation to generation, from one black family to another, by word of mouth and sleight of hand. It is rich in both history and variety of flavor.

To cook soul food you must use all of your senses. You cook by instinct but you also use smell, taste, touch, sight, and particularly, sound. You learn to hear by the crackling sound when it's time to turn over the fried chicken, to smell when a pan of biscuits is just about to finish baking, and to feel when a pastry's just right to the touch. You taste, rather than measure, the seasonings you treasure; and you use your eyes, not a clock, to judge when that cherry pie has bubbled sweet and nice. These skills are hard to teach quickly. They must be felt, loving, and come straight from the heart and soul.

Ah, but when you taste good soul food then it'll take hold of your soul and hang your unsuspecting innards out to dry. It's that shur'nuf everlovin' down-home stick-to-your-ribs kinda food that keeps you glued to your seat long after the meal is over and done with, enabling you to sit back, relax, and savor the gentle purrings of a well satisfied stomach, feeling that all's right with the world. Yes suh! As the good Baptist minister says every Sunday morning, "Yes suh!"

Let me give you a for instance. Say you fry up a batch of fresh chicken to a golden-brown crispness, but you keep the insides so moist, so tender, that all that good juice just bursts forth with the first crunchy bite. Then maybe you bake up some cornbread and buttermilk biscuits, ready to smother with freshly churned butter; and you cook up a big pot of collard greens and pot likka seasoned with ham hocks, onion, vinegar, red pepper flakes, and just enough hot sauce to set fire to your palate. Just a little fire though! Now you pile on a mound of slightly chilled homemade potato salad and fill a pitcher full of ice-cold lemonade ready to cool out that fire. And when you've eaten your way through all of that, you finish it off with a healthy hunk of pecan pie topped with a scoop of homemade vanilla ice cream. Now, tell me the truth—do you think you could move after a meal like that? Only for second helpings, of course!

But that's just the fun-loving, toe-tapping, belly-busting, knee-slapping, thirst-quenching, foot-stomping side of a cuisine that has its more serious side too. For the basic framework of this style of cooking was carved out in the deep South by the black slaves, in part for their white masters and in part for their own survival in the slave quarters. As such, it is, like the blues of jazz, an inextricable part of the black Americans' struggle to survive and to express themselves. In this sense it is a true American cuisine, because it wasn't imported into America by immigrants like so many other ethnic offerings. It is the cuisine of the American, if you like. Because what can't be cured must be endured. As John Egerton so aptly puts it in *Southern Food:*

> In the most desolate and hopeless of circumstances, blacks caught in the grip of slavery often exhibited uncommon wisdom, beauty, strength, and creativity. The kitchen was one of the few places where their imagination and skill could have free rein and full expression, and there they often excelled. From the elegant breads and meats and

sweets of plantation cookery to the inventions of Creole cuisine, from beaten biscuits to bouilla-baisse, their legacy of culinary excellence is all the more impressive, considering the extremely adverse conditions under which it was compiled.

Rations were usually once a week, on Saturday nights, and then the righteous jubilation would commence in the slave quarters. The slaves pretty much insisted on having Sundays as their day to worship. Of course, no alcohol was allowed . . . The slaves had their own way to lift up their souls. They would pray, they would sing, and they would eat![2]

FROM *SOUL FOOD*, PP. 1–2

Soul Music

PETER GURALNICK, JOURNALIST

Soul music is Southern by definition if not by actual geography. Like the blues, jazz, and rock 'n' roll, both its birth and inspiration stem from the South, so that while Solomon Burke, one of the very greatest of soul singers, is a native of Philadelphia, and Garnet Mimms, a little appreciated but nearly equally talented vocalist, made many of his recordings there, the clear inspiration for the styles of both is the Southern revivalism that fueled such diverse figures as Elvis Presley and Hank Williams on the one hand, Little Richard and Ray Charles on the other. I do believe there's a regional philosophy involved here, too, whether it's the agrarian spirit cited by Jerry Wexler ("There was always this attitude, 'Oh, man, we're gonna lose our soul if we do that. We're not gonna let machinery kill our natural Southern thing.'") or simply the idea that Dan Penn, the renegade white hero of this book, has frequently expressed: "People down here don't let nobody tell them what to do." Unquestionably the racial turmoil of the South was a factor, and the rapid social upheaval which it foreshadowed; in fact, the whole tangled racial history of the region, the intimate terms on which it lived with its passions and contradictions, played a decisive role in the forging of a new culture, one which the North's polite lip service to liberalism could never have achieved. Ultimately soul music derives, I believe, from the Southern dream of freedom.

It is not, however (contrary to most received opinion), a music of uninhibited emotional release—though at times it comes close. What it offers, rather, is something akin to the "knowledgeable apprehension," in Alfred Hitchcock's famous definition of suspense that precedes the actual climax that everyone knows is coming—it's just nobody is quite sure when. Soul music is a music that keeps hinting at a conclusion, keeps straining at the boundaries—of melody and convention—

that it has imposed upon itself. That is where it is to be differentiated from the let-it-all-hang-out rock 'n' roll of a cheerful charismatic like Little Richard, who for all the brilliance of his singing and the subtleties of which he is capable, basically hits the ground running and accelerates from there. It is that which, with equal claim to inspiration from the church, rarely uncorks a full-blooded scream, generally establishes the tension without ever really letting go, and only occasionally will reveal a flash of raw emotion. This is not because Motown singers were not equally talented or equally capable of revealing their true feelings; it is simply that Motown was an industry aimed specifically at reaching the white market, and every aspect of that industry was controlled, from the grooming and diction of its stars to the subtlest interpolations on its records. Southern soul music, on the other hand, was a haven for free-lancers and individualists. It was a musical mode in which the band might be out of tune, the drummer out of time, the singer off-key, and yet the message could still come across—since underlying feeling was all there. Feeling dictated the rhythm, feeling dictated the pace; that is why soul remains to this day so idiosyncratic a domain. One of the most common fallacies of a postapocalyptic age such as ours is that there is no room for anything but the dramatic gesture; modulation is something as unheard-of as self-restraint. Soul music, which might in one sense be considered a herald of the new age, knew differently in the 1960s, and among the most surprising aspects of going back and listening to the music today—among its most enduring qualities—are the quiet moments at the center; the moments of stillness where action stops and "knowledgeable" anticipation takes over. Think of the great screams you've heard from everyone from James Brown to Wilson Pickett; think of the fervor of Solomon Burke's or Jo Tex's preaching on subjects as far removed in substance and seriousness as "skinny legs and all" or the price that love can exact. In gospel music, the progenitor of the style, a singer is often described as "worrying" the audience, teasing it, working the crowd until it is on the verge of exploding, until strong men faint and women start speaking in tongues. This is commonly referred to as "house wrecking."

FROM *SWEET SOUL MUSIC*, PP. 6–8

At this point you may be wondering what all this talk of soul food, soul stealing, and soul music has to do with your spirituality. I find important ingredients in the Black experience that seemed to have slipped past many Whites. The pain and agony of slavery kept American Blacks closer to their spirituality, as that was the only way they could survive. In time, that deep inner throbbing oozed out as belly-busting, knee-slapping cooking as well as guitar-plucking songs.

One of the reasons that all-white churches often lose their appeal is because they no longer elude the basic human emotion that rips forth in "house wrecking" songs. One of the avenues that we all must go down to find spiritual abundance is labeled "Emotion-poppin' Lane." Oh yes, some of the brethren will be upset by that suggestion, but they still need to take a long stroll.

Tragically, the consummate English poet Francis Thompson (1859–1907) anticipated the twenty-first century's hunger for God in more than one way. In a period before the devastating power of opium and morphine were fully understood, Thompson became a drug addict. The sensitive mind and soul of the poet could not escape the ravages of his addiction. But even more, Thompson came to understand that no condition of debasement would escape the pursuit of the love of God. He was a man who yearned for and needed spiritual vitality. The following excerpt from Thompson's monumental poem is the final plea of his desperate soul—and perhaps, some of ours as well. Yet, greater than his longing was the love of God, forever pursuing Thompson and us.

The Hound of Heaven

FRANCIS THOMPSON

(1859–1907)

I fled Him, down the nights and down the days;
    I fled Him down the arches of the years;
I fled Him down the labyrinthine ways
    Of my own mind; and in the mist of tears
I hid from Him, and under running laughter.
        Up vistaed hopes I sped;
        And shot, precipitated,
    Adown titanic glooms of chasmed fears,
From those strong Feet that followed, followed after.
        But with unhurrying chase
        And unperturbed pace,
Deliberate speed, majestic instancy,
        They beat—and a Voice beat
        More instant than the Feet—
"All things betray thee, who betrayest Me."

        I pleaded, outlaw-wise,
By many a hearted casement, curtained red,
    Trellised with intertwining charities;
(For, though I knew His love Who followed,
        Yet I was sore adread
Lest, having Him, I must have naught beside;)
But, if one little casement parted wide,

The gust of His approach would clash it to.
Fear wist not to evade, as Love wist to pursue.
Across the margent of the world I fled,
And troubled the gold gateways of the stars,
Smiting for shelter on their clanged bars;
Fretted to dulcet jars
And silvern chatter the pale ports o' the moon.
I said to Dawn, Be sudden; to Eve, Be soon;
With thy young skiey blossoms heap me over
From this tremendous Lover!
Float thy vague veil about me, lest He see!
I tempted all His servitors, but to find
My own betrayal in their constancy,
In faith to Him their fickleness to me,
Their traitorous trueness, and their loyal deceit.
To all swift things for swiftness did I sue;
Clung to the whistling mane of every wind.
But whether they swept, smoothly fleet,
The long savannahs of the blue;
Or whether, Thunder-driven,
They clanged His chariot 'thwart a heaven
Plashy with flying lightnings round the spurn o' their
feet:—
Fear wist not to evade as Love wist to pursue.
Still with unhurrying chase
And unperturbed pace,
Deliberate speed, majestic instancy,
Came on the following Feet,

And a Voice above their beat—
"Naught shelters thee, who wilt not shelter Me."

FROM *MASTERPIECES OF RELIGIOUS VERSE*,
EDITED BY JAMES DALTON MORRISON, PP. 57–61

◆

How can we best satisfy this contemporary hunger for spiritual reality? Many things could be said, but possibly Francis Thompson said it best: "Naught shelters thee, who wilt not shelter Me." Without the reality of Jesus Christ, all other answers and remedies are incomplete and never completely adequate. They all come short. I must seek *Him*.

Is there meaning pumping out there in the world? Sure. But the real question is, how deep is the well from which it springs? A shallow reservoir may work well in the winter but dry up as the hot summer comes. I can find a limited sense of satisfaction in what I see, touch, taste, and feel—but I can't find spiritual vibrance there.

As the stream flowing from the past has blended with what was coming toward me from the future, I have found that I must remember that what matters most is what—or who—is at the center of that swirling vortex. Should nothing stand there, then chaos will spill all over my life. If it is Jesus Christ, then the streams will flow together and become a river filled with meaning and purpose.

If I want a shelter against the problems of tomorrow, then I must offer Him shelter today.

PART TWO

❖ ❖ ❖

Connecting:

Finding Ourselves

SIX

Finding God's Thumbprint

$\mathcal{I}$s there any word out there for the victims of the soul eaters, prey of the spiritual cannibals devouring spiritual vitality these days? Is there a message of hope to be spoken into the moral vacuum that seems to be sucking society under?

Sam Keen isn't very optimistic. In his book *Fire in the Belly*, he says, "With the postmodern man we reach a point where moral reasoning gives out. Once we abandon the age-old quest for consistency, for forging a single identity, for a unifying vision, we are left with no guiding principle except to follow the dictates of the moment."[1]

No consolation there; only confirmation of our fears.

And yet there is a surprise. Lack of direction sent me back to ancient sources for a more profound fountainhead of encouragement, and no book has greater antiquity than the Holy Bible. Rediscovery of reading the Scriptures has always resulted in the recovery of direction, purpose, and moral certainty. I found this to be personally true! Today, multitudes are turning again to what the Bible and centuries of Christian experience reveal about finding spiritual abundance.

Since only the Creator can fully explain the creation, revelation is the singular hope for ultimate insight into this mysterious entity so crucial for our well-being. While living the Christian life, I had come to believe this fact, but the problem was that I had lost touch with how personally important it was to live this truth. I had to return to the Scriptures and start using the *fact* in a *personal way*. Here's what the Bible reminded me that I had to practice.

In this chapter, we turn to the Old Testament story of two thousand years of searching for spiritual abundance. In the next chapter, we investigate how the coming of the Christ became the spiritual compass for the quest. The three subsequent chapters are the insights of the Church Fathers of the first four centuries who explored and expanded upon the teachings of the apostles.

For twenty centuries the Holy Bible and Christian tradition have been the beacon lights along the shore leading us on through dark and foggy nights of confusion. Scripture describes itself as a "lamp unto our feet." No source could be more helpful and reassuring to us in finding spiritual direction.

If. . . if we can figure out what it means.

And that's not as easy as it might sound. For the past fifty years, the American church has struggled with the problem of biblical illiteracy. Churches are filled with people who *believe* but have no idea about what they're supposed to *believe in*. While the Bible remains a bestseller at the corner book store, it goes unread in most of our homes. In the place of solid, inspired teaching, we insert personal opinions that make us feel comfortable but are about as enduring as the wind blowing across the top of our houses. The truth is that we know very little about what the Bible teaches concerning spiritual vitality.

In the next two chapters, we are going to depart from the format of the rest of the book in order to better understand what the Scriptures tell us. Scripture passages along with commentary allow us to put one foot in the ancient world while keeping the other foot in our time. Parallels from contemporary experiences serve as a wall against which we can bounce our thoughts and feelings.

In this sea of troubled souls in which we daily swim, we need a lifeline. Let's look again for the guiding principles and unifying identity we so desperately seek today. Can we find a point of contact and once again touch the hand of God? No matter what it takes, the plunge has to be made to find spiritual vitality.

Where does the human story start? What makes us different from the animals? God breathed the need for spiritual connectedness into *Homo sapiens* and history began:

> This is the account of the heavens and the earth when they were created in the day that the Lord God made earth and heaven. Now no shrub of the field was yet in the earth, and no plant of the field had yet sprouted, for the Lord God had not sent rain upon the earth; and there was no man to cultivate the ground. But a mist used to rise from the earth and water the whole surface of the ground. Then the Lord God formed man of dust from the ground, and breathed into his nostrils the breath of life; and man became a living being.
>
> —Genesis 2:4–7 NASB

Animals were created but not breathed upon. The Hebrew words for *soul* and *breath* are essentially synonymous. We owe our being and uniqueness to existence in a God-permeated atmosphere. As I pondered that insight, I wondered if a portion of my own problem came from living too often outside of that climate.

Like the natural atmosphere in which we live,

the breath of God fills us, sustains us, surrounds us, and maintains our existence. As one would have a hard time explaining water to a goldfish, in the same way, the breath of God is both unavoidably obvious and a complete mystery—just like the meaning of spirituality.

The Old Testament story suggests we go on living when we lose our sense of God's having breathed life into us, but our uniqueness disappears. Animal dimensions gain ascendance over the original purposes of God. A spiritual famine sets in, and we stand on the threshold of the death of our humanity.

LIFE IN THE BLOOD

Every moving thing that is alive shall be food for you; I give all to you, as I gave the green plant. Only you shall not eat flesh with its life, that is, its blood. And surely I will require your lifeblood; from every beast I will require it. And from every man, from every man's brother I will require the life of man. Whoever sheds man's blood, by man his blood shall be shed, for in the image of God He made man.

—Genesis 9:3–6 NASB

The Old Testament described life and the soul as being intricately involved with the bloodstream. Similar to the loss of breath, as blood drains away, so the soul departs and spiritual vitality is gone. Because of this relationship, the Old Testament developed an elaborate sacrificial system to ensure forgiveness of sin and the restoration of vitality to the soul.

The book of Leviticus prescribed animal sacrifice to restore humanness to God's errant people. The Hebrew people believed any action that separated the person from a vital relationship with God was tantamount to death. Subsequently, offering of life was required to counteract the death of the soul and restore spiritual vitality. Consequently, temple worship was the means by which personal restoration was achieved.

———◆———

For the life of the flesh is in the blood, and I have given it to you on the altar to make atonement for your souls; for it is the blood . . . that makes atonement for the soul.

—Leviticus 17:11 NASB

———◆———

The Old Testament foresaw the need for a "suffering servant" to rise out of Israel to complete what was lacking in this system. Through his own blood and pain, this servant would fully accomplish the redemption of lost souls and the recovery of spiritual connectedness, returning them to the fulfilled relationship with God that He intended. The suffering servant would complete what was lacking in animal sacrifice.

Therefore, I will allot Him a portion with the great, and He will divide the booty with the strong; because He poured out Himself to death, and was numbered with the transgressors; yet He Himself bore the sin of many, and interceded for the transgressors.

—Isaiah 53:12b NASB

If the loss of spiritual relationship equals death, is it any surprise that today in the Western world we are living in what is often called "a culture of death"? Without a means of restoration of the soul, the ambiance of life continues to evaporate.

With cannibals lurking on our TV screens and human massacres reported daily on the evening news, we desperately need to get in touch with our

own losses. Just exactly where does one find spirituality? In the bloodstream? A special pocket in the
brain? Is the soul distributed throughout the body?
Could we find a place where a surgeon could cut
with a knife? Or where a researcher could place
electrodes? Because our age looks to science for
ultimate answers, we assume anything that is real
must have a location.

What hints does the Old Testament give us? Can
the stories of the Bible pinpoint the seat of the soul?

Sometimes the Scripture sounds as if the soul is
linked to the place of passion. In Genesis 34:38 and
the suggestion seems to be that the soul is linked to
human desire. Another view is that the soul is a part
of the affections, much like the heart is used sym-
bolically on Valentine's Day.

However, in other passages the soul seems to
have something to do with willpower. We might
wonder if our ability to be intentional is what the
soul is about. First Samuel 30:6 seems to suggest
this conclusion.

On the other hand, other passages sound as if the
soul is connected with sorrow and sadness. Examples
can be found in passages like Ezekiel 27:31 and Job
27:1–4.

Sometimes the head seems to be the command
station for the soul. The book of Daniel speaks of
dreams arising from the soul and "passing through

the mind" (Daniel 2:27–28). The blessing from father to firstborn son is given by putting hands on the head to connect with the soul.

On the other hand, the heart appears more often to be the center of life. The psalmist often cries out for the Lord to examine the heart and mind in an effort to find restoration of the soul (Psalm 26:1–3; 102:1–4).

In Hebrew worship, unique symbolic ornaments were worn to call attention to the special place the heart had in approaching God. The chest piece had a jewel for every tribe in Israel (Exodus 28:29–39). The high priest carried the people of God next to his heart.

The unusual chest jewelry offers us a clue as to what was going on in Hebrew minds. In a pre-psychological age, the heart was used to express the personal dynamics of emotion and motivation. Pain and joy, happiness and despair arise and coalesce in the heart. The heart represented the totality of the experience of life. The Old Testament suggests that both memory and conscience are also found in the heart.

If we take these verses and a host of other passages as our road map, they leave us with the impression that the location of the soul moves around inside us. As we look for locale, the terrain only shifts and becomes more mysterious. The Old

Testament leaves us with quandary and indecision. As I rethought these passages, I came to the conclusion that location is not exact. The Scripture doesn't seem to be interested in answering our question about place.

Since this seems to be the case, let's try another door. Could the Old Testament have been describing a *function* rather than a *place*? Could suggestions of location be used metaphorically? When Hamor said his soul longed for Dinah, his expression was of passion. Aaron's breastplate over his heart was symbolic. Might the soul express itself from time to time more forcefully by coming from different places on the human landscape?

Because Hebrew language is unusually concrete, word pictures are generally used to suggest abstract concepts. Rather than saying the Jews were stubborn, Scripture says "they were a stiff-necked people." Consequently, we might consider a different perspective on talk about body parts and places. I found that the Bible isn't as concerned with *place* as with *function*.

The important issue is discovering how I can operate with a higher level of spiritual vitality. What I need in getting from one day to the next is staying in touch with this source of greater spiritual reality.

The music of blues musician Robert Johnson asks the same questions about function. The longing sound of his music expressed a yearning to find lost spiritual vitality. Arising out of the despair, dejection, and emptiness of life on the Mississippi Delta, the passion of his music was a quest for answers to a desperate inquiry about life, hope, and purpose. I think there's some insight for us in what Greil Marcus observes:

> Blues grew out of the need to live in the brutal world that stood ready in ambush the moment one walked out of the church. Unlike gospel, blues was not a music of transcendence; its equivalent to God's grace was sex and love. Blues made the terrors of the world easier to endure, but blues also made those terrors more real. For a man like Johnson, the promises of the church faded; they could be remembered—as one sang church songs; perhaps even when one prayed, when one was scared not to—but those promises could not be lived. Once past some unmarked border, one could not go back. The weight of Johnson's blues was strong enough to make salvation a joke; the best he could do was cry for its beautiful life. "You run without moving from the terror in which you cannot believe," William Faulkner wrote in one of his books about the landscape he shared with Robert Johnson, just about the time Johnson was making his first record, "toward a safety in which you have no faith."[2]

Heavy breathing and hot blood are what the songs of Johnson were all about, and he was convinced spiritual vitality was still needed out there somewhere. Blues music is certainly not as primitive as the Hebrews in the desert, but the issue isn't antiquity, it's life. I don't agree with some of Marcus' evaluation. Obviously, no one makes "salvation a joke," but Marcus puts me in touch with why the blues sound touches people so deeply. It's a secular cry for what God has already given.

When we look at the Old Testament prophets and psalmists through the end of a trumpet, a number of things come into perspective. The issue isn't anthropology but passion, not religious form but capacity to go on in the face of overwhelming odds.

Moses, Robert Johnson, and William Faulkner wanted to know if God was in there someplace. Johnson and Faulkner gave up on God; Moses insisted that God won't give up on us. I'll stick with Moses.

In this sense, we get a new twist from what old agonizing Jeremiah was about. The recovery of one's spiritual capacity begins when the heart turns back to God, regardless of how tough the road has been.

> "For I know the plans that I have for you," declares the LORD, "plans for welfare and not for calamity to give you a future and a hope. Then you will call upon Me, . . . and I will listen to you. And

you will seek Me and find Me, when you search for
Me with all your heart. And I will be found by you,"
declares the Lord, "and I will restore your fortunes."
—Jeremiah 29:11–14 NASB

Let us push on, with the sounds of Robert Johnson's guitar playing in the background and the
haunting pain of his music hanging in the air, to see
if there is some answer for people who aren't sure
that the promises of the church can be lived out.
They need the same help we're searching for. Here is
a sample of the Old Testament's response to the
need for a little soul music.

Hear my prayer; O Lord; let my cry for help
come to you. Do not hide your face from me when
I am in distress. Turn your ear to me; when I call,
answer me quickly. For my days vanish like smoke;
my bones burn like glowing embers. My heart is
blighted and withered like grass; I forget to eat my
food.
—Psalm 102:1–2 NIV

O God, hasten to deliver me; O LORD, hasten to
my help! Let those be ashamed and humiliated who
seek my life; let those be turned back and dishonored

who delight in my hurt. Let those be turned back because of their shame who say, "Aha, aha!"

—Psalm 70:1–2 NASB

Listening to these passages reminds me that the inner quest for spiritual reality is expressed through the heart. Nothing abstract here, the cry arises from the slave huts on the banks of the Nile—and the same shacks on the Mississippi's muddy banks. And the answer comes back:

Do not fret because of evildoers, be not envious toward wrongdoers. For they will wither quickly like the grass, and fade like the green herb. Trust in the Lord, and do good . . . Rest in the LORD and wait patiently for Him.

—Psalm 37:1–3, 7 NASB

Behold, the eye of the LORD is on those who fear Him, on those who hope for His loving kindness, to deliver their soul from death, and to keep them alive in famine.

—Psalm 33:18–19 NASB

Soul food, indeed! Stronger than fried green tomatoes and barbeque! With that taste in our mouths, let's return to the Hebrew perspective again. What hope is there for people when their spiritual abundance has been gobbled up by conflict and desperation? How do we get back in touch?

Scripture paints a word picture of the Spirit of God sweeping across the globe like the coming of a mighty tempest. Nothing can stand against His coming. We are able to get in touch again if we know and remember that as the blowing wind brings change, so the Spirit of God returns again and again to creation, surging through His people and bringing change. *We have to stand where the wind is blowing.*

Only the Spirit of God revitalizes depleted spirituality. The breath of God returns vitality and rejuvenation to His people. Even when Israel was thoroughly corrupt and justly set aside from her mission, God did not leave His people to suffocate in their iniquity. Once the breath of God returns, life follows. Both individuals and nations are reborn. Spiritual abundance overflows.

Reconnected to the Spirit of God, we discover capacity beyond anything we could have dreamed possible. Spiritual abundance is more than a recovery of connectedness. Significant strength, ability to achieve, guidance, and awareness are imparted and should be expected. Remember the story of Samson? Here are examples for us.

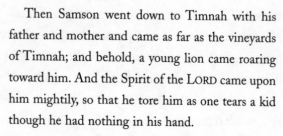

Then Samson went down to Timnah with his father and mother and came as far as the vineyards of Timnah; and behold, a young lion came roaring toward him. And the Spirit of the LORD came upon him mightily, so that he tore him as one tears a kid though he had nothing in his hand.

—Judges 14:5–6 NASB

When he came to Lehi, the Philistines shouted as they met him. And the Spirit of the LORD came upon him so mightily so that the ropes that were on his arms were as flax that is burned with fire, and his bonds dropped from his hands. And he found a fresh jawbone of a donkey, so he reached out and took it and killed a thousand men with it.

—Judges 15:14–15 NASB

When the breath of God is moving, inspiration spills over in unexpected ways. Indeed, as the prophecy to Saul was fulfilled, a similar experience came to David when he was being pursued by Saul.

The same soldiers sent to capture David were turned into prophets. Bystanders found their souls were equally empowered.

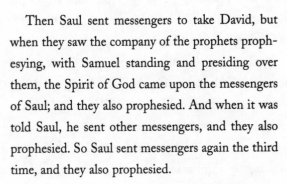

> Then Saul sent messengers to take David, but when they saw the company of the prophets prophesying, with Samuel standing and presiding over them, the Spirit of God came upon the messengers of Saul; and they also prophesied. And when it was told Saul, he sent other messengers, and they also prophesied. So Saul sent messengers again the third time, and they also prophesied.
>
> —1 Samuel 19:20–21 NASB

Something of great significance is happening in each of these stories. When God breathes, new life and possibility follow. People become more than they were before—or thought they could ever be. No joking about salvation here. Far from "pie-in-the-sky and by-and-by," the Old Testament stories of soul recovery are amazing affirmations of human potential.

Why so?

The Image of God

The Hebrew writers perceived the soul to be a function more than a place. In an even larger sense, the *nephesh,* the soul, is not something we possess *as much as a summing up of our total nature.* Scripture suggests the soul is like a mirror held before the face of God, reflecting His image.

Loss of soul obscures our ability to "look like" our heavenly Father, our Creator. Recovery of the soul restores the image of God in us. Writers of Scripture recognized how crucial recovery is.

What are we supposed to be like? The Bible tells us a highly significant truth. The best way to study humankind is not anthropology, but theology. Not by looking at ourselves, but by pursuing God do we find out who we are meant to be. Recovery of perspective grants us powers and spiritual vitality beyond anything we previously dreamed possible.

The image of God is His thumbprint on our lives. The closest the modern age has come to this inspired concept is the idea of the ego. However, the Old Testament's sense of personal unity still eludes our time. Today we are considered to be what Freud called a conscience, a superego, an id, a personality. The Hebrews knew nothing of dividing us up into pieces of personality, into body and soul. Before God we have a singular unity, because this is the way God is. *The soul is both the center and circumference of our existence.*

When all the aspects of what we call personality combine in a singular quest for God, the recovery of the soul has begun. Spiritual vitality starts to flow. We can rest in the palm of the hand that created us.

Let's put it in terms of the terrain where Robert Johnson and William Faulkner would feel most comfortable. Gert Behanna knew those backwoods exceedingly well. After her recovery from a life of alcoholism, she wrote her autobiography under the pen name of Elizabeth Burns. In *The Late Liz, The Autobiography of an Ex-Pagan,* Gert gives us a Hebrew view of rebirth. She begins chapter 1:

> Death isn't so cut-and-dried as it sounds. In looking back I see now that my life is a series of small deaths. For example, some of me died when, very young, I accepted the fact that my father hated my mother. Some of me died each time I sat on the sidelines wondering what secret you had to know to get the boys to dance with you. And then a great chunk of me died at the first night of my first marriage. After that, it was death after death.[3]

Gert was a dear friend who helped me find spiritual depth. She could do that because of her remarkable ability to reflect the image of God. After twenty-four chapters of describing her journey from debauchery to divinity, Gert ends the story with this description of what it is like to be redefined by the love of God.

———◆———

This is my life today and I would not have it otherwise, only more so. I know freedom from stuff in bottles, from guilt and fear and resentment and material possessions, from the judgment of human beings, myself included. My days are filled with challenge and almost too much drama, but, above all, I am at peace with myself. The only judge I have to make a hit with is the Judge of judges.[4]

———◆———

Countless thousands were blessed by the Great Gert, who spent the rest of her life telling the story of her recovery and helping multitudes find theirs.

Perhaps the leap from the ancient world to ours is not as great as it seems. Clearly, God is still breathing, souls are coming back to life, and we are recovering spiritual abundance.

SEVEN

Life Abundantly

The first century's search for spiritual vitality provides a lofty vantage point. Everything described in the last chapter stands as the backdrop, the great panorama against which the new story unfolds.

The ancient longing for the Messiah came to full fruition in Jesus of Nazareth as the new seekers stood on the shoulders of prophets, priests, and kings to see this new thing God had done. Two thousand years later, I wanted to stand in the same crowd and watch the Savior go past again. I wanted to reach out and touch His robe while His power surged through my body. I, too, desired to once again see the story unfold.

Immediately following the grand announcement to Mary of a most unexpected child, she exclaimed:

My soul exalts the Lord,
And my spirit has rejoiced in God my Savior.

For He has had regard for the humble state of
His bondslave;
For behold, from this time on all generations
will count me blessed.
For the Mighty One has done great things
for me;
And holy is His name.

—Luke 1:46–47 NASB

But the place to begin this story is not with Mary's joy at the exaltation of her own soul as much as with the squalor and poverty of the times, the pain and injustice of everyday life. Jesus was the son of a captive people who were daily annihilated at the whim of their brutal masters. He came as light into a very dark age.

Perhaps we can get a better feel of the dark need by looking to a contemporary Jewish scene strangely analogous to the slaughter of the infants that Matthew records in the second chapter of his Gospel. In the novel *Sophie's Choice*, William Styron states, "I seek the essential region of the soul where absolute evil confronts brotherhood."[1] Styron's narrator, the budding young writer Stingo, befriends a distraught and helpless refugee. He exposes us to the darkest side of spiritual need by introducing Nathan Landau and his captive paramour, Sophie.

Sophie is a displaced immigrant, driftwood washed

ashore by World War II. She is a woman of mystery. As if some foreboding secret lurks just behind one of the smoking crematoriums, Sophie's story of her sojourn in Auschwitz is never quite complete.

Stingo is intrigued by Sophie's total preoccupation with guilt, a faceless, relentless guilt present in every aspect of her life. Stingo concludes that the woman is absorbed in self-loathing.

To describe her condition, Styron quotes the Christian writer Simone Weil: "Affliction stamps the soul to its very depths with the scorn, the disgust and even the self-hatred and sense of guilt that crime logically should produce but actually does not." Sophie has stood before a tribunal in her own soul and been found guilty. She exists in a living sentence of death, empty of spiritual strength.

At the height of the story, we discover why. When Sophie entered the Auschwitz death camp, the Nazis forced her to choose which of her two children would live. In order to save one, she had to sacrifice the other. An innocent victim of all-encompassing evil, Sophie's gnarled and bent existence continues as a perpetual extension of the death camp.

With the smell of smoke in our nostrils and the cries of dispossessed victims like Sophie ringing in our ears, we are better prepared to read of the new soul search that begins in A.D. 33, as Jesus came speaking of a spiritual vitality this world can never give. Scripture claims that He descended into the depths of guilt to once again ascend and set us free. We are also in the region of spirituality where absolute temptation meets redemption. I wanted to stand at that place in my own life. As I reached out to Him from that desolate place, here is what I learned.

THE SOUL MAN COMETH

The Old Testament idea of God had been like a picture frame around the universe, but the portrait of Jesus of Nazareth within that frame put a comprehensible face on the Creator. As Jesus fulfilled the centuries-old hope and promise of a Messiah, He became the picture of what God truly is and a human being can be. In the person of Jesus of Nazareth, time and eternity, humanity and divinity were united and joined never to be separated.

The record is clear. Eyewitnesses proclaimed with enthusiasm and awe, "God was in Christ reconciling the world unto Himself." Completed and fulfilled in Jesus Christ, God's self-disclosure also enlarged their understanding of the human soul. They found new meaning in the words *spiritual abundance*. Because Jesus spoke and taught about the spirituality, the subject became of paramount importance to the Church.

Jesus Christ was Lord over law, sin, and even

death. The demons shuddered and scattered at His word; captives of evil were set free, and the blind had sight restored. He spoke directly to the hopes and dreams of men and women as one who intimately knew the depths of the soul. Jesus proclaimed, "I have come that they may have life, and that they may have it more abundantly" (John 10:10). He clearly had the capacity to revitalize and restore lost spirituality.

The Sophies and Nathans of our time desperately want to know if the story is really true. And if so, how can they find the promise? That was also my question.

Much to our consolation, the New Testament is filled with important insight and guidance for recovering and understanding spiritual vitality. For an account of divine revelation, we eagerly turn to that remarkable story of when the soul of God and humanity met and joined in Bethlehem. I read the Gospel stories again to see if it is still possible for divinity to meet and connect again with our lives in an equally wicked world. Here's what I found the Scriptures promised.

Genuine existence is more than simply being alive. The secular "good life" is not enough to give our time on earth enduring meaning. Affluence makes a poor substitute for significance. Health and wealth crumble in the face of death. We have to find hope on the other side of the graveyard.

Recovering our spirituality through the Christ is the only path to fullness, direction, hope, and vitality—beyond the funeral home, in short, *to life*. Jesus said:

> "I am the door; if anyone enters through Me, he shall be saved, and shall go in and out, and find pasture. The thief comes only to steal and kill and destroy; I came that they might have life, and might have it abundantly. I am the good shepherd; the good shepherd lays down His life for the sheep."
>
> —John 10:9–11 NASB

New life in Christ has more than temporal significance. A vital force is released that can be found nowhere else because eternal life is not automatically ours but must come as a gift from God. Only as the heavenly Father grants us this wonderful hope for an eternal tomorrow can we know that our future is secure.

Jesus tells us a paradoxical and surprising thing about finding the spiritual vitality that gives us strength to continue on in the face of death. He said:

> Anyone who loves his father or mother more than me is not worthy of me; anyone who loves his son or daughter more than me is not worthy of me; and anyone who does not take his cross and follow me is not worthy of me. Whoever finds his life will lose it, and whoever loses his life for my sake will find it. He who

receives you receives me, and he who receives me
receives the one who sent me.

—Matthew 10:37–40 NIV

Only when we are completely ready to lose our
lives and confront what seems to be certain death, do
we actually find eternal life. Only then can the
surrendered life truly encounter God, the Father and
Creator, the Son, and the Holy Spirit. That's when
we receive the spiritual strength we must have for
our journey through this world.

ETERNAL LIFE

In contrast to the ideas of Plato and the Greek
world, eternal life was not simply a "permanent possession" that humanity automatically carried forward
after death. Only through one's relationship to the
Christ is there a recovery of spiritual empowerment
that brings the assurance of immortality.

Truly, truly I say to you, unless a grain of wheat
falls into the earth and dies, it remains alone; but if
it dies, it bears much fruit. He who loves his life
loses it, and he who hates his life in this world will
keep it for eternal life. If any one serves me, he must
follow me.

—John 12:24–26 RSV

Jesus tells His disciples that He alone is going to pioneer the way to eternity for them. Of course, they cannot grasp this idea until after they see Jesus on the cross, which He foretold in this passage. However, this way of sacrifice applied to them as well. The disciples had to discover the center of true life! Spiritual abundance was found along the path of self-denial, ending at the feet of Jesus Christ.

In all of these passages, Jesus Christ promises fullness of life *now*. At His touch, we are renewed, and life is extended into eternity. In contrast to the Greek idea of body and soul separating at death, Jesus promised a fullness of life *today*. The life Jesus brought was for the here and now, not just the there and then. Fulfillment begins at the moment spirituality is recovered.

THE VICTORY THAT OVERCOMES THE WORLD

Will the usual scene at the average church on Sunday morning give us a full understanding of the difference Jesus made for the dying, dispossessed people of His time? We struggle with such overpowering issues as whether this year we must settle for the Toyota rather than the BMW or Lincoln. We wrestle with rising health care costs, not the fact that untreatable infection will inevitably lead to amputation and probably death. The average church member is praying to prosper, not just to survive.

Again we have to get in touch with a more critical life-and-death moment to grasp the power of redemption and perseverance offered through the ministry of Jesus of Nazareth. Generally, our mundane problems don't draw deeply enough on the wealth of empowerment which He brought to reveal the potential of the eternal life that is ours in Christ.

For an image and a parable of what the teaching of Jesus promises today, let's return to Auschwitz and a story of another critical choice.

The first time I visited Auschwitz, it was near the end of January. Even the sun looked frozen in the dull gray sky. Wind and freezing humidity turned the unbearable temperatures into a thousand ice picks that poked through anything I wore. Even though I was well-prepared for the winter day, my toes still ached and my fingertips burned. The subfreezing temperatures were almost impossible to endure.

The death camp has been well-preserved, and most of the buildings are still as the Nazis left them. The crematoriums almost look ready for use again; the showers for gassing unsuspecting victims are just as they were when the last Jews crumpled to the floor.

Several of the dormitories have been turned into museums. Piles of marked bags and luggage against one wall are stacked as if their owners will return to pick them up before leaving. On the opposite side of the room, empty green cans of Zyklon-B gas remind us they won't.

Another room is divided by a sheet of glass holding back an avalanche of human hair clipped from Jewish bodies. At one end behind the glass exhibit are several bolts of cloth on display. The Nazis, experimenting with possible uses of the tons of hair, had made the material from the locks of the dead.

Just a few feet away is Father Maximilian Kolbe's cell. Maximilian Kolbe was forty-five years old when he entered Auschwitz for the crime of publishing unapproved material. The SS told him the life expectancy of a priest in the camp was one month. The priest had endured under impossible circumstances.

I stood out on the open assembly ground at the exact place where the prisoners assembled each day, and tried to feel what winter mornings on this spot must have been like. With my fur hat and sheepskin coat on, I had far too much insulation to get an accurate idea. I took the heavy overcoat off. In a matter of seconds, I wondered how anyone *ever* survived.

On one of those torturous mornings, someone had escaped. To discourage escapes from the camp, the Nazis had a rule that if someone escaped, ten men would be killed. When one of the men was selected, he begged for mercy. He had a wife, children, responsibilities; but the plea meant nothing to his captors.

To the amazement of the assembly of guards and captives, Father Kolbe stepped forward as the pleading prisoner was being prepared for death in a torture cell. The priest said, "Let me take his place. I am old. He has a wife and children."

Death didn't follow at the execution wall where so many were shot each week. Father Kolbe was returned to an isolation cell to have the life slowly squeezed out of him—left to fade away in agony without water or food. To the consternation of the guards, courage and perseverance oozed through his pores. He prayed, sang, and recited the Breviary. Father Kolbe died with a smile on his face, his eyes open and fixed on some distant vision. Observers were left with the distinct impression that Father Kolbe, not his tormentors, was in control.

Five decades later, the priest is not remembered so much for the overwhelming pain he endured as for the sense of life he exemplified. He endures as a symbol that once Jesus Christ imparts life to a person, courage, valor, virtuousness, and magnanimity follow. Such development of personhood is *life indeed!*

When Death Comes Early

Jesus' teaching of spiritual abundance was always proclaimed in the face of death. In the first century, men did well to get beyond their thirties; every family left a child buried somewhere. In an age long before the development of anesthesia and antiseptics, penicillin and X-rays, there was a natural urgency to know if life was going anywhere. The multitudes gladly heard the prophet from Nazareth.

As goldfish have no idea what water is, people simply accept life as their natural condition of existence. Perspective is lost on what we have until the time comes when the meaning of life is gone. Jesus warns that at that point of awareness we are already dead. Like fish happily swimming in contaminated waters, the clarity of the blue water is only an illusion. Death floats at our side disguised as normalcy.

And judgment is inevitable. The Scriptures told me that the future of our current situation depends on how we publicly relate to Jesus Christ. Final judgment will only reveal the judgments happening everyday. These moments of truth expose our spirituality and its true condition. What emerges is not a "something," which floats away from the body at death, but the bearer of life itself. The deepest truth about who we are is eternally displayed.

People foolishly believe life is their own to do with as they please. Aren't we the captains of our fate? The masters of our own destinies? Jesus taught that such arrogance only leads to the loss of the soul and death. Quite to the contrary, we are only stewards of the gift of life. At any given moment, an account of this precious loan may be required. Judgment can't be avoided.

To Look Death in the Eye

What does it mean to come to the moment when one confronts the hard, cold reality of personal mortality? How does it feel to rub hands and press the flesh with the grim reaper? As an answer, the New Testament presents us with a cross. The modern world has other forms of agonizing death to make the same point. Elie Wiesel offers a view of the grave from his own reflections on life, barely surviving in the death camp at the edge of eternity.

Wiesel was but a boy when his family was deported from Hungary to Auschwitz and later on to Buchenwald. His parents and sister never returned. His classic remembrance, *Night*, won the 1986 Nobel Peace Prize. The final pages of the book describe the last days before liberation and his release. Ironically, three days later Elie ate bad food and ended up with food poisoning that nearly finished him off.

After days of agony in a hospital, the survivor was able to get on his feet and peer into a mirror. He had not seen his reflection since leaving the ghetto. Wiesel wrote, "I wanted to see myself in the mirror hanging on the opposite wall. I had not seen myself since the ghetto. From the depths of the mirror, a corpse gazed back at me. The look in his eyes, as they stared into mine, has never left me."[2]

Perhaps, such a moment of insight is necessary to understand the truth about our very limited and fragile existence. We need a similar experience to remind us of how short our lives actually are.

What does Jesus tell us is our hereafter? As new life permeates us, what form does our future existence take? To the Greeks' hope of immortality, Jesus said, "No." Instead, the Master promised physical resurrection.

Luke clearly wrote to a Greek audience. He wanted the followers of Plato to correct the misconceptions of their teacher. Luke's gospel, generally considered to be written later in the first century, carefully made his point with a clever literary device. Do you see what is missing in the following passages, compared with what you read earlier?

"I tell you, my friends, do not be afraid of those who kill the body and after that can do no more. But I will show you whom you should fear: Fear him who, after the killing of the body, has power to throw you into hell. Yes, I tell you, fear him . . ."

Then he said to them all: "If anyone would come after me, he must deny himself and take up his cross daily and follow me. For whoever wants to save his life will lose it, but whoever loses his life for me will save it. What good is it for a man to gain the whole world, and yet lose or forfeit his very self? If anyone is ashamed of me and my words, the Son of Man will be ashamed of him when he comes in his glory and in the glory of the Father and of the holy angels."

—Luke 12: 4–5; Luke 9:23–26 NIV

See what's left out? Matthew's earlier allusions to body and soul have been trimmed away. Luke doesn't want the Greeks to misconstrue Jesus' teaching to mean a soul is going to be punished after death once the body is jettisoned. Notice what he says in Acts:

Seeing what was ahead, he spoke of the resurrection of the Christ, that he was not abandoned to the grave, nor did his body see decay.

—Acts 2:31 NIV

He avoids any idea of a soul being left in hades by returning our attention to the bodily resurrection of Jesus.

Luke is particularly concerned with demonstrating that the Easter story is an account of a resurrected body. Earlier in his gospel, he described an afterlife episode, putting great emphasis on bodily appearance and shape. The spiritual abundance that Jesus gives us encompasses all that we are and can ever hope to be.

The rest of the New Testament builds on this idea of our being the bearers of true life, the carriers of spiritual abundance. The apostle Paul was a Jew with one foot planted in the Greek world. He had gone through the ancient world proclaiming new life in Christ and wanted the new believers to know that conversion renewed one's life and future existence.

The apostle knew that an encounter with Christ radically changed everything about one's life. Look what had happened to him! Paul no longer saw people in the same light. He knew the extraordinary nature of how they could be changed.

> Therefore, from now on, we regard no one according to the flesh. Even though we have known Christ according to the flesh, yet now we know Him thus no longer. Therefore, if anyone is in Christ, he is a new creation; old things have passed away; behold, all things have become new.
>
> —2 Corinthians 5:16–17 NKJV

Paul believed these wonderful things are possible because the Holy Spirit brings new life to us.

Our spirituality is the point of contact where eternal life begins through our relationship with Jesus the Christ.

And what does this promise look like in terms of ectoplasm, skin, muscle, tissue, and bone? What is the nature of the shape this spirituality is to take in eternity? With what substance did Jesus Christ present himself on Easter morning? We do well to be humble and tentative in our answers. When Paul wrote of a spiritual body, he was not referring to immaterial matter but to a person filled with the Holy Spirit.

Paul wrote in rather ethereal metaphors suggesting that we will in some way be changed into a form that is everlasting. Here's how he described that transformation:

> For the perishable must clothe itself with the imperishable, and the mortal with immortality. When the perishable has been clothed with the imperishable, and the mortal with immortality, then the saying that is written will come true: "Death has been swallowed up in victory."
>
> —1 Corinthians 15:53–54 NIV

Once again the death camps of World War II unexpectedly offer us a final image, not of death but of what the promise of transformation looks like.

111

Millions of people have been inspired by the story of Corrie ten Boom's journey through Ravensbruck. She and her sister Betsie faced the same indignities and torment that Sophie, Father Kolbe, and Elie Wiesel knew. Tragically, Betsie did not survive. Still, Corrie remembered the amazing discovery the morning one of the inmates forced her to look into the dispensary. Corrie wrote:

> She seized me again, led me to the washroom window, and pushed me in ahead of her. In the reeking room stood a nurse. I drew back in alarm, but Mien was behind me.
>
> "This is the sister," Mien said to the nurse.
>
> I turned my head to the side—I would not look at the bodies that lined the far wall. Mien put an arm about my shoulder and drew me across the room till we were standing above the heart-rending row.
>
> "Corrie! Do you see her?"
>
> I raised my eyes to Betsie's face. *Lord Jesus—what have You done! Oh Lord, what are You saying! What are You giving me!*
>
> For there lay Betsie's face. Her eyes closed as if in sleep, her face full and young. The care lines, the grief lines, the deep hollows of hunger and disease were simply gone. In front of me was the Betsie of Haarlem, happy and at peace. Stronger! Freer! This

was the Betsie of heaven, bursting with joy and health. Even her hair was graciously in place as if an angel had ministered to her.[3]

———————◆———————

Betsie's story is a parable revealing that our present sufferings simply can't be compared to what is ahead. Such was the teaching of Jesus.

When I looked back over my life, I could see many ups and downs. I've had some excellent moments and some extremely painful times. Nevertheless, I can clearly see that the best days were when I was fully in touch with what Jesus said, even if the times were hard. We began this chapter by asking if we have any answers for the Sophies and Nathans of this world. I can tell you emphatically that we do.

I was the first minister to walk through the rubble of the Murrah Building in Oklahoma City on the day of the terrorist bomb explosion. During my ministry I've stood beside hundreds of caskets, including those of my mother, father, and grandmother. I know what the hardness of empty pain feels like. Nevertheless, something almost undefinable but very important happened to me at those moments. During those days, I became like a villager in Nazareth, reaching out and touching the

Master as He walked by. And one touch was always enough. I could tell anyone, everywhere that Jesus Christ imparts spiritual abundance to His friends.

I found that He doesn't stop.

EIGHT

Christians Discover Spiritual Abundance

During the first three hundred years of the Christian era, the growing church attempted to clarify and understand the faith that the apostles passed on to their successors before A.D. 100. Scripture and tradition arose together in a world filled with mystery religions, mystic and esoteric cults vying for the heart and mind of the age. The era was highly speculative, confused, and rife with immorality, strife, and lost people. Into this struggle the Christian message came as a light in a dark night.

The spiritual descendants of Socrates, Aristotle, and Pythagoras were well-entrenched and highly respected teachers of the day. Other long-forgotten proponents of far more bizarre ideas roamed the back streets of Rome, Athens, Jerusalem, and Antioch,

offering their unique brands of salvation. Philosophical and intellectual combat was as fierce as the
world wars of our time. As the dust of argumenta-
tion settled, new names surfaced. Pagan ideas were
confronted, challenged, and defeated. Christian
spiritual intellects like Justin Martyr, Irenaeus,
Athenagoras, Clement, and Tertullian took the
stage. Each of these inspired voices added harmony
to the melody line penned by the hands of the apostles. Later generations recognized their insights as
the church's greatest theological treasures. The
Church Fathers quickly became the master guides
for anyone seeking spiritual reality.

Just as our age is preoccupied with questions of
psychology, their age was gripped by the quest for
discovering God. With one foot planted in the world
of the apostles and another in the Greco-Roman
Empire, these theologians were only a stone's throw
from the days of Jesus. After Scripture, we listen
more intently to their voices than any others. For
them, apostolic succession was not a tradition but a
matter of personal relationship that extended back to
the hand of Christ. They, indeed, have much to tell
us about spiritual abundance. I wanted to know
everything that they could tell me about living the
fullness of the life Jesus Christ brought to this world.

The following excerpts are from these early
apologists, teachers, preachers, and guardians of the

faith called the Ante-Nicene Fathers. These thinkers are the most significant writers before the great Nicene Council convened in A.D. 325. Because the earliest texts are in a foreign prose reflective of classic Greek style, the message is often obscured by the convoluted manner in which they wrote and argued. Therefore, I translated the ancient texts into a contemporary form with language somewhat like *The Living Bible*. Rather than seeking scholarly precision, the insights of the Ante-Nicene Fathers are offered in speech familiar to our ears. Such was the same reasoning that caused the first writers of the New Testament to use Koine Greek, the language of the street, rather than Classical Greek. No attempt has been made to keep these writings in their exact original order either chronologically or structurally; they have been rearranged to present the subject matter in the clearest light.

We return again to a world deeply immersed in questions about spiritual reality and abundance. These excerpts are the opinions of those people who walked with the people who had walked earlier with Jesus and His twelve. They can help us discern the true path from false ones and keep us from wandering down blind alleys. Listen to their voices and see what you find.

God Must Be the Starting Point
TERTULLIAN

At the moment of Socrates' death, all of his so-called wisdom really came from assumptions rather than confirmed truth. Who really knows anything about what is true *without God?* And how can anyone find God *without Christ?* Can anybody understand Jesus Christ *without the Holy Spirit?* Is the Holy Spirit knowable *without the gift of faith?* Obviously not! Socrates was inspired by a very different spirit from another dark place.

Some said Socrates had a demon from his boyhood. Because the teaching of the power of Christ hadn't come yet, there was nothing available to Socrates to ward off the influence of evil. So, if the pagans proclaimed Socrates the wisest of all, how much greater is Christian wisdom that sends all the demons running?

From God you may learn about that which you get only from God. Nowhere else can you receive only what God gives. Who is going to reveal what God alone has hidden? It's better to depend on what the heavenly Father reveals to us than to rely on human wisdom simply because someone like Socrates makes bold assumptions.

The trouble with philosophers is that they disagree on more than they agree about, and when they come up with a truth, they fail to recognize God as the true source of all knowledge. They pretend to be helped by falsehood or lies supporting their claims. They argue around every side of the question while teaching contrary to our standards of faith. What they don't miss of the truth, they infect with their own poisonous ideas . . . Only God's inspired standard of truth is of help.

The Christian needs only a few words for a clear understanding of the subject. After all, the apostles forbade "endless speculations." No final solution can be found by men; only what is learned from God will be the sum and substance of the matter.

Paul saw where this false philosophy would lead when he was in Athens, where he had a bellyful of arrogant pseudo-intellectuals. Such teaching is like wine diluted with water.

FROM *A TREATISE ON THE SOUL*

God Is Our Source

LACTANTIUS

Plato's arguments about the soul contribute much to discussion, but they actually add nothing to truth because he didn't understand anything about the real purpose of God's larger scheme of things. He recognized the truth about the survival of the soul but didn't realize the mystery and place of this idea in God's larger plan. On the other hand, we don't teach by doubtful surmising but because our teachers received divine instruction.

Plato reasoned that anything with perception that moves is immortal; he reasoned that without a beginning to the source of motion, the soul won't have any end to its vitality. Unfortunately, this argument would grant eternal life to the animals, which can't even talk. Confronted with this problem, Plato added the argument that humans' souls are all the more immortal because we can learn, think, remember, invent, foresee the future, and have other skills the animals don't possess. Thus, Plato thought the dissolvable part of humans goes to the ground at death, while the unity of the soul is released from this fleshly prison and goes to heaven under its own steam.

Pythagoras had the same sentiments as well as his teacher, Pherecydes, who also influenced Cicero. These are eloquent speakers, as was Dicaearchus, Democritus, and certainly Epicurus. But even Tullius, who summarized all of their teachings, finally admitted he had no idea what was really true. He concluded, "Only God knows what is reality." Interesting, isn't it? God really is the very source of *our* truth.

FROM *THE DIVINE INSTITUTES*

Spiritual Reality
ORIGEN

The soul of God may be understood as the only begotten Son of God. For as the soul moves and has control over everything in the body, so the only begotten Son is the very Word and wisdom of God, directing the power of God in this world. The soul of God, Jesus, came into our world of affliction, humiliation and tears, entering into our pain. Whenever the Scripture speaks of His suffering, the experience is described with the word soul. "Now is my soul troubled; my soul is sorrowful, even unto death; no man takes my soul from me, but I lay it down of myself." Therefore, it appears that the soul mediates between the weakness of the flesh and the willingness of the spirit.

FROM *ORIGEN DE PRINCIPIIS*

———— ◆ ————

While some of what Tertullian, Lactantius, and Origen wrote sounds convoluted in our time, as I read and wrestled with these texts, I could see how men and women filled with spiritual abundance were confronting the errors of their day. They had found a new source of direction and inspiration. The revelation of God guided them, not philosophical arguments even from the greats like Plato. Origen's reflection on the soul took the reader inside the spirituality of God. Quite a trip!

These writers helped me see in a new and different way that God was calling me to fight the same battle in my time . . . using the same weapons they used! As I attempted to enter that warfare, I found that a new sense of spirituality arose within me.

Here's more of what they said.

TERTULLIAN

We are born with purity, but that immediately comes under attack by the evil one, who looks at all souls with envious eyes. From the very portals of birth, the evil spirit springs into action to entrap us. Idolatry was the midwife assisting at each of our births.

FROM *A TREATISE ON THE SOUL*

METHODIUS

We come into this world with a beauty that is not unlike divine wisdom. The human soul is most like the God who begot and formed us reflecting the image and likeness of the Father, the countenance of an immortal and indestructible shape. The soul's unbegotten beauty is without beginning, not corruptible or changeable, doesn't age or need anything. The Creator encompasses everything with His power and made us after His own image. Of course, the result would be unsurpassed beauty.

Therefore, evil spirits love the soul and plot to defile the Godlike image. Their intent is analogous to the condemnation Jeremiah heaped on Jerusalem. "By the roadside you sat waiting for lovers, sat like a nomad in the desert. You have defiled the land with your prostitution and wickedness." The devil and his angels are vile lovers whose intimacies pollute the mind. They try to cohabit with the soul already promised to God.

FROM *THE BANQUET OF THE TEN VIRGINS*

IRENAEUS

The soul isn't life any more than the body is the soul, but both partake of the life that comes from God. This is why the Bible says of the first human being, "He became a living soul." Therefore, life and the soul are two different things. The soul goes on living and enduring because of the touch of God imparting perpetual duration.

FROM *IRENAEUS AGAINST HERESIES*

Reading these writings taught me that the Church Fathers hungered for God like our society craves spending money. Possessed with a magnificent obsession to know the heart of the almighty Father, they often thought of spirituality as the means or way to find this relationship. The ancient leaders knew that spiritual abundance would be found only as they walked with the Almighty.

Their message was about an inner journey to the place from which God's wonderful reality would bubble forth. Only from deep within are we able to find the way to such a life of spiritual reality. As I quested after the recovery of my own spiritual well-being, I discovered that I had to develop the inner side of my life. Within the silent, quiet recesses deep in my spirit I could at any moment find what Irenaeus called "the touch of God." The real problem was getting quiet enough to reach that internal refuge. As I looked around, I heard the clamor and roar of cars, machines, radios, and a thousand-and-one noise boxes. Most of the people at church were equally noisy.

Once I got to the place of inner quiet, one touch from Christ could take me through an entire day.

Here's more of what the early Christians taught me.

The Importance of Being Human
TERTULLIAN

The fact that internal organs don't detect the existence of the soul doesn't mean anything. Many kinds of nonmaterial entities affect the body. Sound comes into the ear, color goes into the eyes, smell travels up the nose. You can't hold any of those experiences in your hands either. Therefore, the lack of specific shape doesn't give rise to any particular conclusion. As the body is nourished by physical substance, the soul is fed by spiritual food . . .

Chrysippus must have been hallucinating when he claimed two bodies can't be contained in one in order to refute the nature of the soul. Every day, pregnant women give birth to one, two, or even three babies. One Greek woman had four! Even the creation witnesses to how the soul can reside in the body.

We can forget about philosophers' objections. The Gospels offer clear evidence about spiritual reality. Luke's story of Lazarus and the rich man in hell are absolute evidence that the soul goes forth in a material form. The torments of hell wouldn't make any sense unless people had a bodily shape. What resides in hades after departure from the body and waits for the Day of Judgment? Is the soul just a "nothing" in this subterranean world? It certainly is nothing unless it has bodily shape and substance. Punishment and reward require a body . . . An incorporeal thing has no capacity to suffer or to feel anything.

We don't know of any other shape but a human form . . . The inner man is different in some ways from the outer, but they are still one person. The inner must have its own special eyes and ears allowing people like the apostle Paul to encounter the Lord.

FROM *A TREATISE ON THE SOUL*

Spirit and Soul
TERTULLIAN

Some argue that the body contains a spirit of a different composition from the soul. No, the spirit is to the soul like breath is to a person. Their argument is based on the idea that all animals have lungs and windpipes. But it's nonsense to compare the human soul to the workings of a gnat or ant . . . One can't split soul and spirit apart because they can't be divided. We are on much firmer ground to believe that soul and spirit are one.

FROM *A TREATISE ON THE SOUL*

During this period of personal search in my own life, I was seeking a deeper sense of personal unity, an integration of the pieces of the past into the present moment. As I searched for spiritual maturity, I also wanted to be as whole as I could possibly be. When I first studied Plato and company in college, his dissertations on body and soul didn't say much to me. I knew that the Greeks divided people up into parts, but the knowledge didn't ring any bells. They were only ancient ideals.

Years later as I read the Church Fathers, bells went off in my head. I realized the implication of the fact that Christians do not believe in chopping people up in parts. Jesus Christ had brought a new wholeness to whoever would receive the gift. Part of the spiritual abundance He gave the world was the ability to assimilate one's life with new and significant unity. Through Jesus Christ we can become whole people. Such integratedness is our contemporary way of talking about what the ancients meant in their discussions about spirit and soul. In their time, these Christian people sought exactly what we're looking for today.

I could quit searching and trying to find out what the pieces of personality meant. While it was helpful to understand the mind and the emotions, I don't have to use psychology or philosophy to find a sense of well-being. The message of the ancient Church was clear. Through Jesus Christ I could obtain the wholeness needed for personal peace.

During this time of searching, as we discussed in the previous chapter, I was also struggling to understand the meaning of evil in our world. One can't live long without realizing that another destructive dimension exists around us. We may make many bad decisions, but we also have help along the way.

I found that I couldn't study history without being forced to see the demonic dimension that had always existed in the human story.

As I studied the Church Fathers of the first three centuries, I found that they agreed and had important comments on these facts. One commentator noted that probably one of the reasons that the Christian faith became the strongest religious *and political* force in the Roman Empire was because they were the only religion with the capacity to defeat evil. The Christians alone were able to cast out demons in a time rampant with evil. As I read, I discovered that part of what spirituality accomplished empowered us to live far *above* evil.

Listen again to these ancient voices.

◆

TERTULLIAN

When we say there are demons (since we alone cast them out of men's bodies and thereby obviously prove their existence), some disciples of Chrysippus start to get bent out of shape. Yet their attitude only proves the reality and the distasteful nature of the subject. Satan, the angel of evil, is the source of error and contamination in the world luring people into disobedience . . . He is the destroyer!

FROM *THE SOUL'S TESTIMONY*

ORIGEN

The Physician of our souls knows everything necessary for our spiritual health. If, through excessive eating and drinking, we cause our own bad health, we expect to take unpleasant and painful medicine. A terrible condition may require amputation. The worst problems have to be burned out of the flesh. How much more will the soul doctor care about the defects caused by sin and crime? Punishment of fire may even be needed for those who have become emotionally and mentally unstable. Scripture warns that God uses similar methods to redeem us. Deuteronomy 28 threatens fevers, colds, and jaundice, as well as other ailments to get our attention. Other passages greatly expand the list of possibilities. The lapsed, as well as those who have fallen into everyday forms of sin, can expect to drink from God's cup of fury . . . However, God's concern purifies the soul. Remember, fire is for healing! Isaiah said, "The Lord will wash away the filth of the sons and daughters of Zion, and shall purge away the blood from the midst of them by the spirit of judgment, and the spirit of burning." . . . The Bible also says, "The Lord will sanctify in a burning fire." Malachi wrote, "The Lord sitting will blow, and purify and will pour forth the cleansed sons of Judah."

FROM *ORIGIN DE PRINCIPIIS*

How do we get rid of evil distractions? I found that the Church Fathers had a wider range of answers than I would have expected. Tertullian offered prayer and the intercession of a person gifted with the ability to cast out evil. Origen had an approach of a different order, suggesting the struggles that I had to endure were part of the way in which God was purifying me.

Don't misunderstand me. I'm not saying that every struggle is an attack on sinfulness. Often we have experiences that are tragic and not a part of God's plans. People may turn on us because they listen to gossip and innuendos. Sure, bad things happen to good people. However, Origen offered another very important insight. Our daily struggles may reflect the way in which God is cleansing our lives in order that we may receive greater spiritual vitality than we've ever known before. The battle is to make us whole!

I wouldn't have suspected that the problems that I had endured were part of a divine plan to make me more whole and sound. Much to my surprise, I found that I should try to thank God and praise Him even for the hard times. Difficult days can result in a purified character!

LACTANTIUS

If people despise virtue and throw themselves away on lusts, they will eventually be smashed into the ground. In contrast, those who seek the highest things of God will not be enslaved to the earth but will gain eternal life.

FROM *ON THE WORKMANSHIP OF GOD*

LACTANTIUS

When we have offended, we must immediately confess, repent, and seek pardon from God. Repentance is a great comforter and healer, curing old wounds and offering safe harbor. We must always be ready to be obedient to the Lord. Humility is dear and precious in His sight. If the Lord accepts back both a sinner and a haughty man who confesses, how much more will God restore the just person who repents of error? Such a person will be exalted in proportion to his or her humility! True worship is the offering on the altar of God the pledge of our own minds.

FROM *THE EPITOME OF THE DIVINE INSTITUTES*

ARNOBIUS

We have been taught by the greatest teacher that our souls are always close to the snapping "jaws of death." Yet if we study to know Him, the Supreme Ruler, His kindness will sustain us longer in this world because the knowledge of God is a vital force that cements life together. Otherwise, everything would truly fly apart.

Fear of death and concern for the ruin of our souls

is worthwhile because we are prompted to hold fast to Him who alone is able to deliver us from eternal danger. Foolish people think their future depends on themselves, and they act like they are gods.

We are highly aware of our weaknesses and know we don't have wings to fly upward. Utter dependence on God is our only hope. Christ has promised eternal life. No one can call us foolish for bowing down and worshiping Him from whom we will receive these blessings. We expect to receive from Christ escape from a death of suffering and then receive eternal life.

Our detractors argue, "If Christ came to deliver unhappy souls from death and destruction, what about the people who died before He came? What became of these unfortunate people?" You can count on the fact that God's kindness is extended to everyone without favoritism. The trouble with such questions is that there are no complete answers. We need to change our arrogant and conceited attitude, so we can learn what Christ would have already taught us if we had been listening.

Another question is hurled back at us: "If Christ came as the Savior of everyone, then why isn't everyone saved?" I answer, "He frees all alike who ask alike." The fountain of life is open to everyone to drink. If anyone thinks he is so smart that he considers the offering of Christ to be ridiculous and meaningless, why should He go on inviting that person to come to the waters? . . .

God neither compels nor terrifies anyone. Our salvation isn't necessary to His well-being, but it surely is to ours.

FROM *ARNOBIUS AGAINST THE HEATHEN*

The earliest Church Fathers taught me that the spiritual abundance Jesus the Christ gave people in New Testament times didn't stop with the death of the apostles. The gifts, ministries, and work of the Holy Spirit continued on through the centuries with as much vitality as the New Testament promised. Thousands and thousands of people bore witness to the fact that they had discovered the source of peace, joy, and well-being. Even as people of our time passionately quest after wholeness, for these believers of the early Christian era, the promise of integrated personalities was fulfilled. Even the claws of evil were clipped and Satan, the roaring lion, was reduced to nothing more than a pussycat.

Jesus Christ remained God's brightest light regardless of how dark the world became. I can rely on Him today with the same confidence and expectancy as these great writers of the past. Times might change, but He won't!

NINE

The Abundance Prevails

The first decades of the third century were an extraordinary time in the history of the Church. After more than one hundred years of persecution and attack, Christians not only gained respectability and acceptance, but the Church also became the foremost institution in the declining Roman Empire. By seeking the well-being of their souls at the expense of their lives, the faithful ended up also gaining the world! Christian abundance was over-flowing.

Supposedly, Emperor Constantine saw a cross in the sky. More likely, he read the handwriting on the wall and recognized the wisdom of paying attention to which way the political tides were flowing. The truth was that Constantine needed the Christians much more than they needed him. In A.D. 313, his Edict of Milan declared an end to all hostilities toward believers. Immediately Church leaders ceased to be sport for the Colosseum and bait for the lions. Bishops, priests, and theologians were sought after by the emperor for their sage advice and godly directives—and ability to keep the ship of state from sinking.

In truth, the badly declining remnant of the once-mighty Roman Empire needed every ounce of political unity that could be mustered. The Church appeared to be the strongest and most cohesive group that might hold things together. In order to appropriate the resources of the Christian community, Constantine carved out a new alliance between church and state. It was given to the Church to sit at the right hand of the emperor. Even though Jesus instructed Pilate that His kingdom was not of this world, Constantine did everything possible to create a new way of doing business.

By this time, ideological controversy was not new to the Church Fathers, for eleven decades having battled serious attempts to erode "the faith once delivered." The word *heresy* simply meant "doctrine contrary to the apostles' teaching," and there had been plenty of that! From the bizarre gnostic ideas of Marcion to the ranting and ravings of the Montanists, no small number of heretical writers had even used the apostles' names as pseudonyms to make their deviant ideas acceptable. The unsettling and disquieting effect of these detours had been a major reason for the compiling of Scripture and the rise of creeds. The traditions, writings, and teachings of the Ante-Nicene Fathers were important road signs for the faithful to follow. But controversy had not ended when Constantine waved the white flag.

The emperor's political sensibilities gave him pragmatic concerns about the colliding religious viewpoints in his empire. Unanimity at the altar meant a better chance for unity at the polls. Constantine's influence became an unexpected source of encouragement for further clarification of how the teachings of Jesus and the apostles were to be understood.

In A.D. 325, the greatest minds of the Christian community were called by the church and state to assemble at the little town of Nicea to hammer out a statement of faith that would guide the empire and the Christian world even to this very hour. The Nicene Creed was to become the most comprehensive and succinct statement the church would ever develop.

Behind the scenes of the frantic wrangling over words and concepts strange to us (gems such as *ousia; homoousia, substantia, persona, essence,* and *being)* was an even more profound concern for the well-being of the Christians. Constantine wanted cohesiveness; the Church demanded fidelity. Believers' souls dined on truth. Verity was not negotiable, lest the eternal future of the faithful be jeopardized by deadly error.

The issue wasn't simply putting words together to make some abstract doctrine sound right. These Church Fathers were concerned that the believers be able to continue to find the spiritual vitality that made their lives so excitingly different. Without right doctrine, they would end up with a dead faith. Christians had been able to overcome the host of wicked forces bearing down on them from every side, and it was essential that nothing impede the source of God's power. The debate at Nicea had personal consequences for these followers of Christ.

Questions were raised from many sources about the nature of Jesus. Strange answers were given. Apollinarians proclaimed that Jesus of Nazareth did not have a human soul. Sabellians erased any line between the Father and the Son, while Arians preached Creator and Christ were of completely different substances. The Photinian heresy stripped away all divinity from the Christ, and the Manicheans argued to the contrary: There was no humanity in Jesus. Such debates were of critical importance to the future of the Church. The stakes were even higher than in the previous century. Spiritual vitality was on the line.

The work of the Nicene Council was conducted with profound seriousness. These issues were larger than mere ideas, more important than whether Plato would prevail over Aristotle, Athanasius over Arius.

Because the Christian fed on God's Word and was nourished by virtue, false teaching could be the equivalent of feeding a baby poison.

The writings of the Ante-Nicene Fathers had been like a great funnel pouring insights and conclusions into this council. After Nicea, the hourglass opened up once again for fresh reflections to flow forth across the empire, based on the new standards for correct doctrine.

Times were different now and new viewpoints could emerge. Once again, we meet the most profound and spiritual minds the Christian community produced. No intellect towers higher than Saint Augustine. From the backwaters of the obscure monastery at Hippo, his writings would reshape the world and become the basis for medieval society, prevailing for a thousand years.

We turn now to the Nicene and Post-Nicene Fathers, voices continuing to speak of things unseen and the meaning of spiritual reality. After A.D. 325, they carry the questions forward, always seeking paths that will take the faithful on to spiritual maturity. Adapted to modern speech and thought forms, their writings still inspire us even after more than fifteen centuries. They want to help us find spiritual abundance.

The Post-Nicene writers built on the foundations laid by their predecessors, further expanding the general view of what spirituality is, does, and becomes in the light of the Nicene Creed. Questions still remained about the Christian life and living it successfully. Here is some of the guidance Augustine and the saints offered for his day . . . and for ours.

———————◆———————

Origins
SAINT AUGUSTINE

The human soul is, in a unique sense, immortal, though not absolutely immortal as God alone is. The Scriptures point out the soul can die. Remember, "Let the dead bury their dead"? Once alienated from the life of God, the soul loses its true life. The soul is not a part of God, or it would be truly indestructible and incorruptible. Of course, mere reflection will tell any of us how limited we are.

Philosophers arguing for the soul's participation in God may say sin is the result of the corruption brought on by the body. So what! If the soul sins, it dies. What difference does it make where the problem comes from? The result is the same. The heavenly Father remains holy, while the soul becomes tainted. God and the soul are two very different matters.

Remember that the soul is immaterial, not a substance. Whether one defines matter as essence, substance, or some other term, it is important for us to know what we are talking about. In order not to be confused, we must be clear that the soul's guidance and direction over the body make its nature immaterial because the soul can't be located as if it resided in one specific place giving out orders.

For example, the mind is not material in the same sense that earth, water, and air are material. The soul has its own unique composition superior to anything in this world. This substance cannot be picked up and identified by any of the senses of the body.

I am convinced that sin comes to the soul purely by its own free will and choices. It is not God's fault or a mistake in the way we were created. Even though we get into trouble because we want to, we can't free ourselves from sin by willpower or self-sacrifice. Only by the grace of God revealed in Jesus Christ can we find salvation. Every single human soul must receive his mediation and sacrament of grace or face the consequences, judgment, and punishment. When we are regenerated in Christ, we become a part of his holy fellowship, the Church, not only surviving the death of this present body but also receiving a new body in glory.

FROM *LETTERS OF ST. AUGUSTINE*

SAINT AUGUSTINE

What is the soul? Think about the subject and reflect. I don't want the credit for these ideas; I want you to find the truth within yourself.

Did I miss something? Are we made only in the image of the Son? Just the Father? Maybe the Holy Spirit? No. Genesis says, "Let Us make man after Our own image and likeness." The Father does not act without the Son, the Son without the Father, and all in concert with the Holy Spirit. "Our image" means we bear the full image of God.

SERMON II OF SERMONS ON NEW TESTAMENT LESSONS

As I worked on translating the writings of Saint Augustine and the other Church Fathers, I found that they often have a hidden agenda. While they want us to be clear about what is true and should be believed, they are also concerned to help us find our way to the personal promises of Christ. Within the folds of their teaching is a driving interest in making sure that we don't cut ourselves off from God's best gifts. Saint Augustine knew that sin can destroy our ability to carry the image of God in our life.

Sin is not breaking a few of God's better rules. Rather, transgression is a full-scale attack on reality. It reduces the truth of God to nothing more than dirt around our shoes. Those who persist on this path soon have so eradicated the image of God in themselves that nothing is left but the face of an animal. The beauty of God's presence has become nothing more than dust.

A strong example of how this process works is the sin of adultery. While a juvenile mind may consider sexual sin as only "fooling around," it in fact erases the beauty of the unique singleness of one's relationship with a mate. The other person quickly becomes only another cog in the social machine. What was intended to last a lifetime disappears, and meaningful love vanishes. These early Christian writers knew that we must be relentless in dealing with the unexpected sin that can pop up in our lives. Look at what they wrote and said.

The Struggles of the Soul

SAINT CHRYSOSTOM

We must face the facts about our own sin. Like a horse that is not completely tamed, we don't like to be saddled with the burden of our guilt; but our reluctance is the work of Satan. We must repent if we are to escape punishment. We can't obtain pardon for our sin if we don't confess. Compassion and kindness await the penitent, but we cannot receive pity until after we are ashamed of our deeds.

FROM *WORKS OF ST. CHRYSOSTOM*, HOMILY XXI

JOHN CASSIAN

Why do we fall into sin? The source of the problem is the corruption of the rational part of the mind and soul, where presumptiveness and conceit emerge. Healing this problem requires humility and a modest perspective on oneself. You will get back on track when you face the fact of how great your need is. Aspiring to be a teacher, you will realize you are still very much in need of a teacher.

We are often tempted and trapped by what seem to be quite reasonable feelings that are nothing more than snares of the enemy. You will remember during the temptation of our Lord in the wilderness, the evil one attacked the three natural affections of the soul. The natural affection of *desire* was challenged by the temptation to turn stones to bread. The will to *power* was addressed by offering the kingdoms of the world. *Reason* itself was engaged by arguing, "if" you are the Son of God, cast yourself down. Nothing availed because nothing was damaged in the Christ. Take heed!

FROM *CONFERENCE OF ABBOT ABRAHAM*

SAINT AUGUSTINE

The soul will either be ruled by reason or error. However, error doesn't guide but destroys.

Remember the story of the Samaritan woman at the

well? She was ruled by the five senses, but error shook her around like a rag doll. Her problem was that she wasn't married to the lover she was living with at that moment. In fact, she had gone through five husbands! When she was honest about her condition, Jesus opened her mind. His conversation with her might be understood from a slightly different viewpoint.

"Your problem is, your five senses ruled your life," He said. "Now you're beginning to get your mind on a higher plane. But sin in your life and relationships is still distorting your thinking. If you get the iniquity out of your life, then you will even understand who I am."

The woman's perceptiveness was distorted by sin.

FROM *ON THE GOSPEL OF JOHN*

SAINT CHRYSOSTOM

I wish I could undress and reveal the souls of those who swear all the time so they could see the wounds and bruises acquired daily because of their foulmouth habit. No one would ever need to say anything to them. The wounds would be more shocking than anything we might suggest.

Since we can't take a peek at the soul, maybe we can look at the rottenness of our thoughts. Remember, Ecclesiasticus 23:10 (the book of Sirach in the Apocrypha) says, "As a servant continually beaten will not be clear of bruises, so the person who swears and names

God continually will not be purified in their soul." The mouth that swears all the time cannot help but frequently commit perjury. Therefore, I beg you to get rid of this wicked habit.

FROM *THE WORKS OF ST. CHRYSOSTOM*, HOMILY XV

Losing Our Souls

SAINT AUGUSTINE

Consider Jesus' meaning when He said, "Let the dead bury their dead." When unbelievers bury a body, both are dead. The one has lost the soul, and the others have lost God. For as the soul gives life to the body, God is the life of our soul. Just as the body expires when the soul leaves, the loss of contact with God brings spiritual death. We can't help dying sooner or later, but the death of the soul is by our choice.

SERMON XII OF *SERMONS ON NEW TESTAMENT LESSONS*

SAINT AMBROSE

Pay attention! We face three possible deaths. The first one is *spiritual*, followed by *natural* demise. Finally, there is a death of *eternal punishment*.

Adam received death both as penalty and remedy. Of course, the world became a difficult place of sweat and toil. On the other hand, death was also given as a cure for the end of this world's evil. I would suggest that you

Christians not think of natural death as a penalty but as a remedy. Therefore, there is good in death because it removes us from the battles going on in this world.

FROM *ON THE BELIEF IN THE RESURRECTION*

SAINT CHRYSOSTOM

Want to know what a dead soul looks like? Remember the story of the rich man and Lazarus, the poor beggar? Now there's a picture for you! The rich man clearly had a dead soul. He ate, drank, and lived only for pleasure. Even now, the unmerciful and cruel are in the same shape. All the warmth of their love and compassion has gone cold, and they are no better than corpses. The problem is no small matter because without these qualities a person is already dead.

FROM *THE WORKS OF ST. CHRYSOSTOM*, HOMILY VI

SAINT CHRYSOSTOM

I have a word for people who recognize no boundaries and take advantage of people and also something to say to their victims. Bear their arrogance generously, for they are ruining themselves, not us. While they defraud us of our money, the cheats divest themselves of the good will and assistance of God. Though clothed with the wealth of the world, such persons are the poorest of all. True wealth lies in being able to say,

"The Lord is my shepherd. I will lack for nothing." Only one thing is required of us. In all things, we are to give thanks to God. On that basis, we have all things in abundance.

FROM *HOMILIES ON HEBREWS*, HOMILY XX

The Attack of Evil

JOHN CASSIAN

No one doubts that evil spirits can and do influence what goes on in our thought life. The attacks begin after demons observe our behavior. Our actions, words, and inferences reveal the openings to our soul. Evil spirits can't possibly touch people who protect the inner recesses of their souls.

Greediness is suggested when we already are acting gluttonous. Fornication becomes a thought after the dart of lust is fixed in the soul. Grief, anger, and rage arise first in the heart and then come out in our actions. Just watch what people do, and you'll be able to see where the spiritual attacks are going to occur.

FROM *FIRST CONFERENCE OF ABBOT SERENUS*

JOHN CASSIAN

We have excellent guidance on the subject of demon attacks on the soul from the blessed Antony (the Egyptian founder of monasticism). From his own experience of leading a holy life, Abbot Antony came to understand the attacks of evil very well. He taught that demons cannot find entrance into the mind, body, or soul of anyone until the soul is first deprived of all holy thoughts, emptying it, and distancing the soul from spiritual meditation.

Unclean spirits respond to humans in two ways. Divine grace makes them subject to believers because of our personal holiness. We can demand they not bother us. On the other hand, the sacrifices and gimmicks of the sinful making offerings to evil spirits will lure them on in their attack on these foolish worshipers of evil. Flattered by attention, they will zero in on such people.

The most savage demons would not even venture to approach Antony when he was making the sign of the cross on his breast and forehead. As he devoted himself to prayer and supplications, the evil spirits returned to where they came from. Christian profession has great power over all fierce and powerful shadows of evil.

FROM *CASSIAN'S CONFERENCE*, CHAPTERS 18 AND 19

As you read the thoughts of these saints, much of what they wrote might sound basic and elementary. But that's exactly why their writings are so important. I found that they kept bringing me back to the issues that I have to deal with in everyday life—basic and elementary problems! I am reminded of the practical concerns that have the capacity to destroy spiritual vitality. These voices from the past remind me that paying attention to my relationship with God is the most important issue that I have to deal with in my life. By the same token, I must treat sin with infinite seriousness. The issue isn't making a mistake, but actually "toying" with death.

Perhaps, at this point you might want to stop reading and think about the implications in your own life. Where do you fall short? What should you be doing *right now* to make sure that everything in your heart is pure and good? Think it over for a few minutes and then read on.

RESURRECTION AND THE SOUL

As I worked with the truths and ideas presented by the Church Fathers, I realized that their insights made my life better and more valid. They knew how to take me to the place where strength, peace of mind, and hope arose within me. If this was all I had to tell you, I can assure you it would be enough.

But there is more.

The Christian faith always points beyond today. Not that this moment isn't sufficient, but the life that Jesus Christ brought to us fully anticipates an eternity that is ahead. With time, that promise took on an ever-increasing meaning and consequence. Here are some additional thoughts that I found in the writings of the Church Fathers.

SAINT AMBROSE

Philosophers who speak of the immortality of the soul aren't very satisfying. They only argue for partial redemption. What good is it if the work of God in us fades with time? What do we have if death is the same for the sinner and the just? What good is a miserable immortality?

Paul said, "If in this life only we hope in Christ, we are more miserable than all people." He wrote those words because God has prepared for us another life reserved as reward. We want out of this world to find a new body. Holy men always lamented the length of their lives in this world. David, Jeremiah, and Elijah moaned about life in this body.

The soul leaves behind this world and the problems of the body to join with the heavenly company in singing the praises of God. With harps they sing together, "Great and marvelous are Your works, O Lord God Almighty; just and true are Your ways, King of the nations."

FROM *ON BELIEF IN THE RESURRECTION*

SAINT AMBROSE

If you won't accept the fact of the Resurrection by faith, look around you at the examples we see in nature. Grapevines, olives, and many other kinds of fruits are witnesses to the ongoing cycle of dying and rising again that comes at the end of the year. The resurrection of the dead at the end of all time is equally appropriate. Otherwise, we would sink back into this evil age. For exactly this reason, Jesus Christ suffered on the cross to deliver us from this wicked world. We would be in a heap of hurt if we had to return to life again just to go on sinning.

Many philosophers denied the resurrection of the body but believed in the immortality of the soul. No one by speculation and reason did or could have come to such an amazing truth. Only revelation from God revealed the resurrection of the body.

FROM BOOK II OF *ON DISBELIEF IN THE RESURRECTION*

We've heard some of this message before echoed from the very first century as Jesus the Messiah called forth believers. We must work at the Christian life. Spiritual abundance isn't an accident but comes as the product of living a disciplined, set-apart lifestyle. We have to take sin seriously. Humility, repentance, sincerity, devotion to Christ, as well as other qualities of the Christian life, are vital for our spiritual well-being. However, the most important dimension is to recognize the breadth of our need. Augustine and company remind us that *we must guard the heart!*

Spiritual abundance is of such proportions that as this life wears out, on the other side of my last breath is a new life of greater magnitude than I can imagine today. The passing of the decades and the centuries did nothing to diminish this promise made by Jesus Christ. His pledge that He came to bring us eternal life was not a "sales job" for the rest of His mission. From the very beginning, the truth was basic and part of the whole of His teaching.

It *was* His gift to me. It *is* His gift to *you.*

TEN

Spiritual Discernment

*L*ong before medieval popes vied with kings for power and influence, the leaders of Christendom were remarkable men and women of extraordinary intellect, spiritual acumen, and overwhelming personal integrity. Gripped by a common quest for a beatific vision of God, preachers, teachers, monks, theologians, martyrs, and laypersons pushed into the frontiers of the soul, seeking the sacred space, the Holy of Holies, formerly reserved for entry only by the Aaronic priesthood, but now open to all through Jesus Christ. No longer concealed from Gentiles by forbidden courts and hanging curtains, the presence of God was open to all who came by the way of the Cross.

Unfortunately, large segments of the Christian community assume the book of Acts is all of the story there is to tell. Even those who know something of the history of the Reformation often comprehend little about the likes of Celtic Christians like Columba and Aidan, or earlier European leaders Irenaeus, Origen, and the eloquent preacher John Chrysostom. Intellectual blindness robs us of the collected wisdom of the greatest spiritual mountain climbers.

The second, third, and fourth centuries of Church history are filled with profound insights into the new life offered in Christ. Behind the intellectual and academic issues raised in those three centuries was a fervent desire to find the way through the barrier separating the world of time and eternity. Convinced that the resurrection of Jesus Christ opened a new path, these early pioneers blazed a trail for the faithful to follow into the spiritual hinterlands.

We turn now to highlights gleaned from their writings. I quickly discovered a road map to lead me across my own barren plains and valleys of despair. Tips from these time-tested travelers lifted me above the empty preoccupations of my own age and offered me sage insight, clarifying the real from the artificial, the profound from the banal, and the significant from the entertaining. At the end of the trail, I once again found the fulfillment of the promises of Christ.

Like mountain climbers gathering around the campfire in preparation for the next day's ascent to the top of the peaks, we can look for the glow of fire and candle reflected in the eyes of these saints who have been to heights of which we have only heard. They know the way to spiritual abundance. Let's find out about their discoveries.

Road Signs and Markers

SAINT CHRYSOSTOM

After an event in the Olympic games, a herald stands up and calls out with a loud voice, "Does anyone accuse the winner? Has there been any cheating?" Character counts in these contests and they aren't nearly as important as what happens to our spirituality. If such examinations are important in contests revealing the capacity of the body, how much more important is it to inquire about the condition of our lives? We face a similar referee calling out, "Only the holy can draw near."

His call isn't about the forgiveness of sins but about personal holiness. The goal is larger than absolution. God wants to know about the presence of the Spirit in our lives and the amount of good works that follow. Not only are we pulled out of the mud, we are meant to be clean and beautiful. Therefore, let us look to the adorning of the soul in golden robes girdled with truth.

FROM *THE WORKS OF CHRYSOSTOM*, HOMILY XVII

SAINT CHRYSOSTOM

Nothing is as contradictory and foreign to the character of the Christian as laziness and being absorbed with this present life. Was your Master crucified to give you a comfortable life? Was Jesus pierced with nails so that you could be affluent? . . . Making a pretense of Christianity while living in ease and luxury is contrary to the message of the Cross.

The soul that serves Christ can't avoid a cross. If we are going to live the crucified life, we will love the Cross regardless of the personal cost. Since our Master was hung upon the tree, we must imitate Him. If no one crucifies you, crucify yourself lest you bring on a spiritual death! Remember, Paul said, "The world has been crucified to me and I to the world" (Galatians 6:14). Baptism is the way of the Cross by which we receive the seal of Christ. Laying on of hands comes through the Cross . . . Jesus identified suffering as the route of the Cross when He said, "Unless a man take up his cross and follow Me, he can't belong to Me." We must be prepared to die.

FROM *THE WORKS OF ST. CHRYSOSTOM*, HOMILY XIII

SAINT CHRYSOSTOM

Prayer is a mighty weapon when it's done right. Remember that continued petition has overcome shamelessness, justice, and even savage cruelty. Recall Jesus' teaching about persistence? He told the parable of a friend who beat on the door of the neighbor until the acquaintance got out of bed in the middle of the night. He said, "Because of his importunity the neighbor will rise and give whatever the man seeks to him."

We must apply ourselves to prayer. When prayer is offered with sincere earnestness and without self-seeking, powerful things happen. Wars have been stopped, and undeserving nations have benefited. God said, "I have heard their groaning and come down to deliver them." Prayer is like medicine; it prevents sin and heals wrong.

We must pray with the humility of the publican crying out, "Be merciful to me a sinner." Then we will obtain everything.

FROM *THE WORKS OF ST. CHRYSOSTOM*, HOMILY XXVII

JOHN CASSIAN

To pray as we should, we must observe the rules. First, we must get over being anxious about worldly concerns. Next, we must put out of mind all care and preoccupation with business affairs. In addition, clear your mind of obsessing about other people's defects, shut out chattering noises, silliness, and certainly get rid of anger. A tendency to be depressed must be cleared up. You had better eradicate lust and covetousness by the roots. Cleanse yourself of anything that gets in the way of simplicity and innocence. You will establish a foundation of humility that will support a prayer tower reaching to the heavens.

The soul must be freed of all distracting conversations and roving thoughts that finally drown out our conversations with God. Don't kid yourself. Whatever you were thinking about the hour before you start to pray will return during your prayers. We have to get mentally prepared before we even start the prayer time. Get your mind focused; then you can pray without ceasing and feed on continual contemplation of almighty God.

FROM *CASSIAN'S CONFERENCE*

JOHN CASSIAN

Another problem we have found in trying to reach the heights through prayer is constant interruption by our colleagues, which keeps us from remaining in uninterrupted silence. During periods of fasting when we are attempting to get the body under control, the arrival of some brother breaks into the advantage we are seeking through this discipline. Unfortunately, too few people understand the value of the solitary life for prayer.

FROM *CONFERENCE OF ABBOT ABRAHAM*

———————◆———————

As I studied John Cassian's comments, a destructive fact loomed before my eyes. I could see the people gathering for worship on Sunday morning in many of the congregations that I work with. I could see them chatting with each other, sharing stories, relating social situations. Across the sanctuary the sound of talking filled the air . . . and killed any possibility for silence and prayer. "Uninterrupted silence" was not the order of the day; uninterrupted conversation was!

I know many good and fine Christians, but I don't know many who pray thirty minutes a day, any day of the week. Simple. Basic. Unfortunately, it just doesn't happen.

And we wonder why spiritual abundance eludes us? I could quickly see that the deficit in our prayer lives was enough of an answer to make us quake.

Few of the early leaders of the Church were more significant than Saint John Chrysostom. In Greek his name literally meant "silver throat." The great preacher understood the importance of a disciplined Christian life and helped the believers of his day find the higher path. The following are some directives he gave to his listeners.

◆

SAINT CHRYSOSTOM

Paul tells us to put on the breastplate of faith and love. He is talking about doctrine. We must have strong protection to keep anything from piercing the heart. Only faith and love will keep the fiery darts of the devil from penetrating. Where the power of the soul is protected with the armor of love, no secret plot of evil will destroy us. Wickedness, hatred, envy, flattery and hypocrisy cannot infiltrate such a soul . . . Paul taught that faith, hope, and love abide. He speaks of how important it is to become strong in these particular areas.

FROM *HOMILIES ON THESSALONIANS*, HOMILY IX

SAINT CHRYSOSTOM

Discipline is important. Even as we age, it is important to maintain the same disciplines we did during youthful days. Aging causes us to lose the encouragement of youthful vigor.

During our youthful days, we were driven by achievement, desire for status, luxury, lust, and the desire to have everything we see. However, old age depletes the body and cripples our desires. Of course, some old men are intractably stubborn even as they approach death and the final judgment. Of course, this problem is an excess of wickedness. So, don't count on old age alone to cover up the sins of your youth.

FROM *HOMILIES ON HEBREWS*, HOMILY VII

SAINT CHRYSOSTOM

We must learn how to face storms. Notice how boat captains are calm and composed when the tempest is raging, while the other people on board are confused and terrified. The pilot sits at the helm calm and undisturbed because he knows the art of sailing. Pay attention and lay hold of the sacred anchor that is our hope in God.

Remember the parable Jesus taught in the Sermon on the Mount about the house built on the sand? When the tumult came, the edifice crumbled. Unless we are ready for storms, our souls are in danger of being destroyed by less than even a genuine tempest. Simple rumor of trouble may do us in. We will end up being even more foolish than the man who built unwisely.

FROM *THE WORKS OF ST. CHRYSOSTOM*, HOMILY XVI

SAINT CHRYSOSTOM

If you say I must live a solitary life to be a good person, you insult virtue. We need to be able to face every difficulty and our souls still prevail. Whether in famine or plenty, the apostle Paul said, "I know how to face abundance and want." Paul gladly took on every difficult circumstance and problem. We should imitate him. We will be the most blessed of people in this life and the next one as well.

Consider a rich man with a wife, children, and every other thing he could want. If he loses all of these gifts and is still virtuous, he is like a rock unmoved by the raging sea. As the captain of a boat laughs during the storm while the children are terrified, so the prepared soul will be tranquil while everyone else is confused. Nothing can disturb the disciplined soul.

FROM *HOMILIES ON PHILIPPIANS*, HOMILY XII

SAINT CHRYSOSTOM

We must give more attention to making our soul beautiful than using any other adornment we pick up. We have the capacity to decorate a house and wear fashionable clothes. Apply the same ability to the soul. Remember, an ugly bride's defects only become more obvious when paraded around in elaborate dress. In the same way, what is gained if you have expensive carpets in your house while your soul goes about in rags, naked and foul? Take care of yourself lest like the bride, you make yourself all the more worthless. When people insult us with words, we are appropriately upset, yet we don't even notice how we offend our own soul by our misdeeds. Although the hour is late, let us come to our senses and give foremost care to our souls.

FROM *THE ACTS OF THE APOSTLES*, HOMILY XXXV

JOHN CASSIAN

The nature of our spirituality could be compared to a feather. If it isn't damaged or soaked, a feather naturally sails up to the heaven with the lightness of breath. In the same way, our souls are meant to sail upward to God. We must make sure they are not damaged by physical lusts but carried upward through our spiritual meditations. We do well to remember our Lord's admonition, "Take heed that your hearts are not weighed down by drunkenness and the cares of this world." Therefore, if we want our prayers to not only go up, but beyond the sky, we must be careful to purge all earthly faults. Then our prayers will rise unrestrained by the weight of any sin.

FROM *CASSIAN'S CONFERENCE*

SAINT CHRYSOSTOM

Tell me, if you had a wonderful and admirable husband who loved and treated you very well, knowing he would not leave you but would give you anything you desired, would you want anything more? Even if you suddenly lost everything but still had such a husband, wouldn't you even think yourself the richer?

So, what are you whining about? Because you don't have a big home? Well, start remembering that your sin has been taken away and you have acquired God's good pleasure. Paul said, "We are blessed when we bear everything with thankfulness." Just consider how blessed you will be when, "in all things you will give thanks." If you lose ten thousand pounds of gold, be grateful. By thanking God in all circumstances, you will acquire ten times ten thousand more blessings.

FROM *HOMILIES ON HEBREWS*, HOMILY XX

SAINT CHRYSOSTOM

To perfect any art, we begin with simple requirements and tender beginnings, gradually building up to the more demanding requirements. Like a boy learning to pronounce the letters of the alphabet, we must push on to become proficient at rhetoric. In the same way, we have to begin with simple principles of prayer and meditation. We begin with only a slight idea of what the laws are. We need help in ever keeping the idea of God before our minds. Our minds always tend to wander and slip off into personal reflections and speculations.

FROM *THE WORKS OF ST. CHRYSOSTOM*, HOMILY XXVII

SAINT CHRYSOSTOM

Let us stretch our minds toward heaven. Held fast by that desire, we seek to be absorbed and immersed by spiritual fire. Anyone filled with the fire of inspiration has no fear of anything, whether wild beast or man.

Armed with fire, this person does not fear traps because he knows danger retreats as he approaches. Such fire cannot be withstood or endured because it is all-consuming.

Let us clothe ourselves with heavenly fire that we may offer up glory to our Lord Jesus Christ, with the Father and the Holy Spirit, to whom be glory, might, honor, now and ever, world without end. Amen.

FROM *THE WORKS OF ST. CHRYSOSTOM*, HOMILY XXXIV

SAINT ATHANASINS

If we choose, we can repent, seek cleaning from our lust, and be cleansed from all defilement in order to read clearly the Word of God. Even if we are immature and the pressures of life get in the way, the creation itself declares who the Creator is through order and harmony. Divine Scripture teaches us we are made in the image of God. It clearly says, "Let Us make man after Our image and likeness." Once the obstacles are removed, the purity of this image can shine forth, and we can become like mirrors, truly reflecting God. We really can attain the image of God Himself, as His personhood was clearly stamped on Jesus, the Son.

FROM *CONTRA GENTES*

DETOURS AND DEAD-END STREETS

As I studied these early Christian writers, I found that their ancient cultures had absorbed a wide range of strange, esoteric, and mystical religious ideas. The coming of the Christ was a confrontation with what Paul called "the doctrines of demons"—evil and intoxicating religious systems feeding on superstitions and flourishing in the darkness. As unlikely as it might seem, in our time we have witnessed a return of some of these notions. We have seen some of these destructive ideas resurrected in the New Age movement. Although they may come with new names, the substance is the same. Such twisted concepts remain blind alleys that we must avoid.

Both the Ante- and Post-Nicene Fathers spoke to the problem of going down the wrong path. They help us keep the present age in perspective. Here are some of their teachings that have a distinctly modern ring.

Reincarnation

IRENAEUS

Our Lord taught not only the continued existence of our souls, but also that they pass from an earthly body to a renewed body, preserving their original form and remembering what happened in this life. Remember the story in Luke 15 of the rich man Dives and the poor man Lazarus in the next life? They clearly recognized each other and remembered the past. Dives wanted to send a warning message back to his relatives from his place of punishment and suffering.

From this story we can conclude: We continue to exist, passing from an earthly to an eternal body; we possess our previous form, memory is retained. Abraham had a prophetic gift, and before the Final Judgment each person's abode will reflect what he or she has coming.

FROM *IRENAEUS AGAINST HERESIES*

IRENAEUS

We can refute the idea of transmigration of souls from body to body (reincarnation) because people don't remember anything about what happened in a previous state. The simple reunion of a soul with the body couldn't possibly extinguish all previous experiences! If transmigration were true, we would have a ton of memories hovering around!

For example, when the body is resting, the soul has no trouble producing dreams and communicating these experiences to the body. If we lived in a previous body for a whole lifetime, we would have many, many more similar recollections.

FROM *IRENAEUS AGAINST HERESIES*

TERTULLIAN

The most damaging philosophers don't care about the spirituality of their students when they teach the idea that the soul enters the body at some time after the person is conceived in the womb. We believe the soul is there at the moment of conception. They suggest the soul enters the fetus before complete viability is reached. They say the human seed is deposited *ex-concubiter* in the womb and then starts to form like bread rising in an oven. Somewhere along the way the soul drops in. The Stoics, Aenesidemus, and at points, Plato himself, all teach this heresy. But even the youngest mother will tell you of the movement of life within her. At the earliest possible moment, she recognizes a real human being is there.

Even pagan astrologers recognize that the soul is present from conception because they made their calculations on the basis of conceptions. Where else would we get our similarities with our parents if not from the seed of the soul?

FROM *A TREATISE ON THE SOUL*

TERTULLIAN

How is a living being conceived?

Remember how John leaped in Elizabeth's womb when Mary came carrying Jesus in her? This response in both women clearly indicated their unborn infants were fully alive. Jeremiah indicated the same when he wrote that God said, "Before I formed you in the womb, I knew you." Was this a dead body Jeremiah spoke of? Certainly not! "God is not the God of the dead, but the living."

We maintain that the body and soul are formed at exactly the same time. They are conceived, formed, and maintained perfectly simultaneously. Not a moment of interval exists in their formation. When we die, the separation is simultaneous. Birth is the same.

FROM *A Treatise on the Soul*

ARONBIUS

Tell us, Plato, why in the *Meno* do you have a young slave answer questions on mathematics as if to prove what we learn actually comes from the memory of a previous life? Such answers don't come from a former life but from intelligence. Simply following the meaning in your questions leads to insight, not prior instruction . . . It's much easier to believe we are learning "something" for the first time than it is to accept the idea that the soul is recalling "something" for the first time.

FROM *Aronbius Against the Heathen*

SAINT AUGUSTINE

What good person could tolerate the idea that a whole lifetime spent in great distress and difficulty, fighting off evil and miseries of every kind, followed by experiencing the bliss of the contemplation of spiritual life, leads to an afterlife where we lose every achievement of the soul and then return to this life to a start *all over* again? Even worse is the idea we might have to make this return over and over again through endless cycles of going from misery to bliss and back to pain! Such ideas make no sense; especially since the more a person loves God, the more that person strives for blessedness. How could we love someone more and more if we thought that at the highest moment of relationship, that person would abandon us? We can't even love human friends if we know they are destined to be our enemies!

FROM *THE CITY OF GOD*

SAINT CHRYSOSTOM

Once the soul is torn from the body, there is no longer any possibility of the soul wandering. The Book of Wisdom says, "The souls of the righteous are in the hands of God." Equally, the souls of the wicked are straightaway led to their end. In the story of Lazarus and the rich man, Christ says, "This day they require your soul from you."

FROM *THE WORKS OF ST. CHRYSOSTOM*, HOMILY XXVIII

Obviously, we need to be discerning people, but to be spiritually discerning is infinitely more significant. As we read what devout seekers wrote centuries ago, their insights help give us an idea of how spiritual discernment looks, feels, and works. Even though what they have written sounds like the thought might have come from a contemporary person, I am encouraged to realize how important that particular insight is when it comes from across the centuries.

At this point in my life's journey, I am impressed to realize how much difference age can make. When I was twenty I didn't even realize some of the critical issues existed that I would have to live through and experience when I was forty. Crossing the line into the fifties added new dimensions and surprises. Breaking barriers to the future across the decades opened new and important doors. Increased discernment followed.

And yet . . . how limited it's all been.

If time does anything, the ticking of the clock reminds me of how little I know, see, and understand. We find ourselves swallowed by fads and investing in gimmicks that later prove to have no future. Only as they fail, do we realize the depth of Saint John Chrysostom's expectation that in eternity we will hear, "Only the holy can draw near." Even though it contrasts severely with this age, becoming more holy is still the most important aspect of discernment that we can pursue today.

Holiness doesn't mean the development of affected ways of dressing, speaking, or appearing in public. The goal is more basic . . . and much more difficult. We are called to put on "the breastplate of righteousness." We cover our hearts and minds with the love of God and seek to become an incarnation of that same profound sense of caring. Guarding our hearts is everything.

No task is more essential than keeping the center of our doing and being pure. From that point springs all discernment.

ELEVEN

The Renewed Quest

*A*fter the fifth century, the civilized world changed abruptly and radically. The political slide Constantine tried to stop turned into an avalanche. Huns, Visigoths, and Germanic tribes poured into the shrinking Roman Empire, destroying the remnants of a proud past. Order became chaos, and darkness descended over the world. By A.D. 590, the temporal power of Pope Gregory I was actually greater than the military of the state.

The sophisticated writings and arguments of Stoics, Platonists, and Christian apologists were no longer intelligible to the growing number of illiterate peasants, trying to scratch out a living under difficult circumstances. Priests celebrated Latin Masses in a language that common people could not read or understand. Form was replacing substance.

That insight caused me to look at my own life in

a different way. What had caused me to feel that I was losing my soul? My spirituality? I was shocked to realize that in all of the good things that I was doing, the right form was pushing the inner substance aside. Not that anything was wrong with the procedures I followed, the way I worshiped, what I did each day, but I had started to live on the surface. My best intentions had only pushed me into the backwaters where spiritual abundance didn't flourish. As I looked at the problem within myself, I realized that I needed to pay more profound attention to what was substantial, to what counted in my own spiritual walk. This realization took me back to a new place, a different place that caused me to read Church history from a different perspective. As I looked at how these ancient Christian writers reacted to their changing times, I found the clues that I needed to know how to better deal with what was changing around and within me.

Across the untamed forests and hinterlands of Europe, monasteries sprang into existence and candles were lit again in the dark night. The travels of Saint Patrick and his disciples left behind new centers of Christian community. An extremely gifted red-haired young man named Crinthann, or "Fox," began an energetic evangelistic foray across the British Isles and on to Gaul. Generally remembered by the name Columba, the monk returned to Ireland, founding more than forty monasteries. The monastery his successor, Aidan, founded at Lindisfarne in northern England became the religious wellspring of all English culture.

A new spirituality was emerging. The medieval era would eventually shift its philosophic underpinnings from a Platonic bent to an Aristotelian orientation. In the meantime, the monastic centers spawned men and women of fervent devotion to prayer, contemplation, and the quest for the beatific vision of God. Leaving behind the worries, woes, and rewards of secular life, monks and nuns gave their undivided attention to the cultivation of their spirituality.

As the Greeks' inquiries into matter, being, and spirit faded, the new quest was more practical. Seekers were searching for an encounter with God. The now prevailing belief in the resurrection of Jesus and His real presence in holy Communion spurred the faithful on in their desire for contact with the life of God. I was reminded that this was where spiritual abundance started in my life. Christian worship had been the well-spring from which personal contact grew.

Building on the instruction of Scripture and the insights of the Church Fathers, the medieval saints left behind a new literature on spiritual abundance.

Their singular devotion to God still lifted me to the heights and challenges found by travelers on the rarified atmosphere of the Spirit. We can follow some of these trails into our own time. Here are some of the writings that inspired me and took my journey down new trails.

---◆---

When in the Fullness of Time
HILDEGARD OF BINGEN, GERMAN PROPHET
AND MYSTIC (1098–1179)

When in the fullness of its time
this creation wilts,
its vigor returns to its own source.

This is the underlying natural law.
When the elements of the world fulfill
    their function,
they come to ripeness
and their fruit is gathered back to God.

Now these things
are in reference to the soul's life:
spiritual vitality is alive in the soul
in the same way as the marrow of the hips
    in the flesh.

Out of the soul in good standing,
the vigor of the virtues flows out
as do the elements of creation,
it flows back in the same capacity in
    attentive prayer.

The soul is a breath of living spirit,
that with excellent sensitivity,
permeates the entire body to give it life.

FROM *MEDITATIONS WITH HILDEGARD OF BINGEN,*
VERSION BY GABRIELE UHIEM, P. 60

The Soul Is Oned to God
DAME JULIAN OF NORWICH,
ENGLISH MYSTIC (1343–CA. 1419)

The soul, that noble and joyful life
that is all peace and love,
draws the flesh to give its consent
by grace.
And both shall be Oned
in eternal happiness.
Our soul is Oned to God,
unchangeable goodness,
and therefore
between God and our soul
there is neither wrath nor forgiveness
because

there is no between.

Because of the beautiful oneing
that was made by God
between the body and the soul

it must be
that we will be restored
from double death.

From *Meditations with Julian of Norwich*
version by Brendan Doyle, p. 31

From our vantage point in the twenty-first century, we can see that these writers used *soul* in many ways that didn't necessarily reflect how the Scripture actually used the word. However, they were not a part of how Plato had once used the expression. Time had given them special ways to talk about spirituality. Now they were writing about the two sides of our existence; the world and God. As I read and reflected on how Christians like Hildegard and Dame Julian used the word *soul*, I was reminded of how essential it is to pay attention to the inner side of my life, to the place where my relationship with God arises and dwells, because this is the realm from which spiritual abundance arises. The following is an example of how this part of the inner life operates.

———◆———

The Interior Guide
Saint teresa of Avila, Spanish Carmelite nun (1515–1582)

I began to think of the soul as if it were a castle made of a single diamond or of very clear crystal in which there are many rooms, just as in Heaven there are many mansions.

While I was beseeching Our Lord today that He would speak through me, since I could find nothing to say and had no idea how to begin to carry out the obligation laid upon me by obedience, a thought occurred to me which I will now set down, in order to have some foundation on which to build.

I began to think of the soul as if it were a castle made of a single diamond or of very clear crystal, in which there are many rooms, just as in heaven there are many mansions. Now if we think carefully over this, sisters, the soul of the righteous man is nothing but a paradise, in which, as God tells, He takes His delight. For what do you think a room will be like which is the delight of a King so mighty, so wise, so pure and so full of all that is good? I can find nothing with which to

compare the great beauty of a soul and its great capacity. In fact, however acute our intellects may be, they will
no more be able to attain to a comprehension of this
than to an understanding of God; for as He Himself
says, He created us in His image and likeness. Now if
this is so—and it is—there is no point in our fatiguing
ourselves by attempting to comprehend the beauty of
this castle; for, though it is His creature, and there is
therefore as much difference between it and God as
between creature and Creator, the very fact that His
Majesty says it is made in His image means that we can
hardly form any conception of the soul's great dignity
and beauty.

It is no small pity, and should cause us no little
shame, that, through our own fault, we do not understand ourselves or know who we are. Would it not be a
sign of great ignorance, my daughters, if a person were
asked who he was, and could not say, and had no idea
who his father or his mother was, or from what country he came? Though that is great stupidity, our own is
incomparably greater if we make no attempt to discover what we are, and only know that we are living in
these bodies, and have a vague idea, because we have
heard it and because our faith tells us so, that we possess souls. As to what good qualities there may be in
our souls, or who dwells within them, or how precious
they are—those are things which we seldom consider
and so we trouble little about carefully preserving the

soul's beauty. All our interest is centered in the rough setting of the diamond and in the outer wall of the castle—that is to say, in these bodies of ours.

FROM *THE INTERIOR CASTLE,*
TRANSLATED AND EDITED BY E. ALLISON PEERS, PP. 28–29

———◆———

Teresa of Avila admonished me to pay attention to the rooms inside my own inner castle, where spiritual abundance arises and is stored. She reminded me that I needed to pay attention to this realm from which life springs. As I read her thoughts, I was reminded how vastly different our society is from her world. Recently, I was in a bookstore and stopped at the magazine rack. Before my eyes were multitudes of periodicals stressing the body, sexuality, personal appearance, attractiveness, etc., but I didn't see one current popular magazine that even talked about spirituality. In our society, someone has to stop us in our tracks to remind us that our current emphasis is on what will soon fade.

Ours is a body-oriented world where many leaders don't even function as if a spiritual side exists. I must periodically stop and recollect how important it is to remember that God loves me in a way that is going to last forever. The "eternality" of who I am is what really counts!

Here's what a medieval German wrote about lasting things.

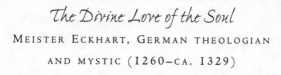

The Divine Love of the Soul

MEISTER ECKHART, GERMAN THEOLOGIAN
AND MYSTIC (1260–CA. 1329)

God
loves the soul so deeply
that were anyone to take away from God
the divine love of the soul,
that person would kill God.

If you were to let a horse
 run about in a green meadow,
the horse would want to pour forth its whole strength
 in leaping about the meadow,

So too
it is a joy to God
 to have poured out
the divine nature and being
completely into us
who are divine images.

FROM *MEDITATION WITH MEISTER ECKHART*
VERSION BY MATTHEW FOX, P. 29

The Rapture of Divine Love

EVELYN UNDERHILL, ENGLISH POET,
NOVELIST, AND MYSTIC (1875–1941)

In one of his most daring passages, the anonymous author of "The Mirror" writes, "'I am God,' says Love, 'for Love is God, and God is Love. And this soul is God by condition of love: but I am God by Nature Divine. And this [state] is hers by righteousness of love, so that this precious beloved of me, is learned, and led of Me without her [working] . . . This [soul] is the eagle that flies high, so right high and yet more high than doth any other bird; for she is feathered with fine love.' . . . "

I think no one can deny that the comparison of the bond between soul and the absolute to "ghostly glue," though crude, is wholly innocent. Its appearance in ["The Epistle of Prayer"] as an alternative to the symbol of wedlock may well check the uncritical enthusiasm of those who condemn at sight all "sexual" imagery. That which has seemed to the mystics appropriate and exact is proved by its reappearance in the next century in the work of a greater contemplative. "Thou givest me," says Peterson, "Thy whole Self to be 'mine whole and undivided, if at least I shall be Thine whole and undivided. And when I shall be thus all Thine, even as from everlasting Thou hast loved Thyself, so from everlasting Thou hast loved me: for this means nothing more than that Thou enjoy Thee in myself and myself in Thee. And when in Thee I shall love myself, nothing else but Thee do I love, because *Thou art in me and I in Thee, glued together as one and the selfsame thing* which henceforth and forever cannot be divided."

FROM *MYSTICISM*, PP. 427–28

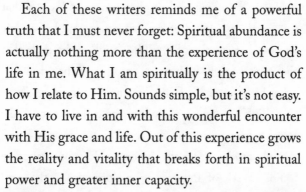

Each of these writers reminds me of a powerful truth that I must never forget: Spiritual abundance is actually nothing more than the experience of God's life in me. What I am spiritually is the product of how I relate to Him. Sounds simple, but it's not easy. I have to live in and with this wonderful encounter with His grace and life. Out of this experience grows the reality and vitality that breaks forth in spiritual power and greater inner capacity.

People who talk about hearing God speak are often called "Christian mystics" as if they are in a special unique category from the rest of the human race. I find that these ancient writers deny that suggestion. The Bible supports their contention that God Almighty wishes to speak to His people and that this is normal. Sure, people differ. Some describe their experiences in more demonstrative ways than others do. Moreover, some people appear to have greater capacity to hear God than others will. We know that in every realm of experience talents and abilities differ. Nevertheless, He chooses the way that is most natural for each of us and speaks in those terms.

Listen to how Thomas à Kempis, a medieval Christian, challenges us to listen to what God is saying.

Christ Speaks to the Faithful Struggler
THOMAS À KEMPIS

"I will hear what God the Lord will speak" (Psalm 85:8). Blessed is the soul which hears the Lord speaking within, and from His mouth receives the word of consolation. Blessed are the ears that catch the pulses of the divine whisper (Matt. 13:16, 17) and give no heed to the whisperings of this world. Blessed indeed are those ears which listen not after the voice which is sounding without, but for the truth teaching inwardly. Blessed are the eyes that are shut to outward things, but intent on things inward. Blessed are they that enter far into things within, and endeavor to prepare themselves more and more by daily exercises, for the receiving of heavenly secrets. Blessed are they who are glad to have time to spare for God, and who shake off all worldly hindrances.

Consider these things, O my soul, and shut up the

door of your sensual desires, that you may hear what the Lord your God speaks in you (Psalm 85:8).

Thus says your Beloved, "I am thy salvation," your Peace, and your Life: keep yourself with Me, and you shall find peace. Let go all transitory things, and seek the things eternal. What are all transitory objects but seductive things? And what can all creatures avail, if you are forsaken by the Creator?

Renounce therefore all things, and labor to please your Creator, and to be faithful unto Him, that you may be able to attain unto true blessedness.

FROM *THE IMITATION OF CHRIST*,
TRANSLATED BY E.M. BLAILOCK

◆

A REMINDER ABOUT BROKENNESS

I found that I simply couldn't read very long until these writers insisted that I face the fact that this world is filled with brokenness. We inevitably sin, and destruction follows. I have to take into account that my best intentions get caught up in the turmoil that arises from my own selfishness and preoccupation with my problems. The result is disaster.

Yes, the bookstore is filled with books on self-mastery, self-improvement, becoming the person you want to be. The list of options goes on and on almost without end. Unfortunately, few of the current trends tell you much more than how to use your natural-born selfishness with greater effectiveness. It's true today; it will be true tomorrow. This "effectiveness" won't last for long.

In contrast, these saints remind us that developing our spiritual abundance demands that we go far below these surface suggestions and face life on the most basic level. Often this journey demands that we look pain straight in the eye. Much to my surprise, I found that facing the issues, people, and situations that hurt me the most proved to be the quickest way to recover spiritual vitality. Betrayal and abandonment are serious issues, but living through them can take us on to the place where growth follows.

Here's what Catherine of Siena can teach us.

The Perfection of Tears
CATHERINE OF SIENA

Do you not know, my daughter, that all the sufferings the soul bears or can bear in this life are not enough to punish one smallest sin? For an offense against me, infinite Good demands infinite satisfaction. So I want you to know that not all sufferings in this life are given for punishment, but rather for correction, to chastise the child who offends. However, it is true that a soul's desire, that is, true contrition and sorrow for sin, can make satisfaction. True contrition satisfies for sin and its penalty not by virtue of any finite suffering you may bear, but by virtue of your infinite desire. For God, who is infinite, would have infinite love and infinite sorrow . . .

Let every soul rejoice who suffers many troubles, because such is the road that leads to this delightfully glorious state. I have told you before that you reach perfection through knowledge and contempt of yourself and knowledge of my goodness. And at no time does the soul know herself so well, if I am within her, as when she is most beleaguered. Why? I will tell you. She knows herself well when she finds herself besieged and can neither free herself nor resist being captured. Yes, she can resist with her will to the point of not giving her consent, but that is all. Then she can come to know that [of herself] she is nothing. For if she were anything at all of herself, she would be able to get rid of what she did not want. So in this way she is humbled in true self-knowledge, and in the light of holy faith she runs to me, God eternal. For by my kindness she was able to maintain her good and holy will steadfast when she was sorely besieged, so that she did not imitate the wretched things that were vexing her.

You have good reason, then, to take comfort in the teaching of the gentle loving Word, my only-begotten Son, in times of great trouble, suffering, and adversity, and when you are tempted by people or the devil. For these things strengthen your virtue and bring you to great perfection . . .

I have told you about perfect and imperfect tears, and how they all come from the heart. Whatever their reason, they all come from this same vessel, and so all of them can be called "heartfelt tears." The only difference lies in whether the love is ordered well or ill, is perfect or imperfect.

I still have to tell you, if I would fully answer your desire, about some souls who want the perfection of tears though it seems they cannot have it. Is there another way than physical tears? Yes. There is a weeping of fire, of true holy longing, and it consumes in love. Such a soul would like to dissolve her very life in weeping in self-contempt and for the salvation of souls, but she seems unable to do it.

FROM *CATHERINE OF SIENA*,
TRANSLATED BY SUZANNE NOFFKE

Another significant difference between these Christians of the past and our present age is their view of discipline. While many believers obviously didn't live out the significance that God had promised them, these stalwart saints knew it was usually because they failed to discipline themselves in the ways that the Christian life demanded. As contemporary weight lifters like to say, "no pain, no gain."

While spiritual abundance is a gift, it also appears as we seek for it. The quest is an important part of the reception. God gives the gift, but He reaches out to the people who are in training to receive His offering. The saints of the past became so important because they paid the price to become spiritually endowed. Their devotion and work at training their inner lives paid off in important gifts that appeared to simply bloom out of the rich soil of their lives. How fertile was their soil as compared to someone else? No one knows. What is obvious is that the discipline they cultivated proved to be everything that God intended for them. Notice this quality in the following writings. The correct use of willpower is urged.

DISCIPLINE AND SPIRITUAL ABUNDANCE

The Dialogue
CATHERINE OF SIENA

Each of you has your own vineyard, your soul, in which your free will is the appointed worker during this life. Once the time of your life has passed, your will can work neither for good nor for evil; but while you live, it can till the vineyard of your soul where I have placed it.

This tiller of your soul has been given such power that neither the devil nor any other creature can steal it without the will's consent, for in holy baptism the will was armed with a knife that is love of virtue and hatred of sin. This love and hatred are to be found in the blood. For my only-begotten Son gave His blood for you in death out of love for you and hatred for sin, and through that blood you receive life in holy baptism . . .

There are, then, two aspects to yourself: sensuality and reason. Sensuality is a servant, and it has been appointed to serve the soul, so that your body may be your instrument for proving and exercising virtue. The soul is free, liberated from sin in my Son's blood, and she cannot be dominated unless she consents to it with her will, which is bound up with free choice. Free choice is one with the will, and agrees with it. It is set between sensuality and reason and can turn to whichever one it will . . . .

FROM *CATHERINE OF SIENA*,
TRANSLATED BY SUZANNE NOFFKE

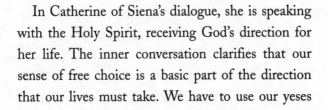

In Catherine of Siena's dialogue, she is speaking with the Holy Spirit, receiving God's direction for her life. The inner conversation clarifies that our sense of free choice is a basic part of the direction that our lives must take. We have to use our yeses and nos in the most constructive ways if we are to keep the inner life clear and pure. When a bad spiritual experience occurs, the reason is because we've made the wrong decision. Sound simple? Basically, it is. However, at the time of the decision, the matter probably sounded extremely complex.

One of the reasons we call these people from the past "saints" is because they had the ability to cut through the nonsense and deal with life in what now looks like simple straightforward terms. Thoroughly good people make everything appear rather simple, while deceptive individuals always appear complex. The seeming simplicity is the result of cutting through to the sacred center and responding as God intended. The longer I studied these writings from the past, the more I hungered to be nothing more than such a simple person.

One of the ways these saints taught was by telling stories that made their point vividly. The following story is an anonymous example of their quest for godliness.

The Pilgrim Soul
ANONYMOUS NINETEENTH-CENTURY
RUSSIAN CHRISTIAN MONK

I said, "But I beg you to give me some spiritual teaching. How can I save my soul?"

For a long time I wandered through many places. I read my Bible always, and everywhere I asked whether there was not in the neighborhood a spiritual teacher, a devout and experienced guide, to be found. One day I was told that in a certain village a gentleman had long been living and seeking the salvation of his soul. He had a chapel in his house. He never left his estate, and he spent his time in prayer and reading devotional books. Hearing this, I ran rather than walked to the village named. I got there and found him.

"What do you want of me?" he asked.

"I have heard that you are a devout and clever person," said I. "In God's name, please explain to me the meaning of the Apostle's words, 'Pray without ceasing.' How is it possible to pray without ceasing? I want to know so much, but I cannot understand it all."

He was silent for a while and looked at me closely. Then he said, "Ceaseless interior prayer is a continual yearning of the human spirit toward God. To succeed in this consoling exercise, we must pray more often to God to teach us to pray without ceasing. Pray more, and pray more fervently. It is prayer itself which will reveal to you how it can be achieved unceasingly; but it will take some time."

So saying, he had food brought to me, gave me money for my journey, and let me go.

He did not explain the matter.

FROM *THE WAY OF A PILGRIM*,
TRANSLATED BY R. M. FRENCH, P. 4

Our contemporary enemy is busyness. I'm sure that most of the readers of this Russian monk's little story thought this suggestion that they pray more often was a good idea, but they don't actually have the time that it takes. I found that pursing the spiritual life while doing Christian work wasn't any easier than working in a secular occupation. Being alone with God takes just as much time for one type of person as it does for another. There are no shortcuts.

The issue demands making the time to be alone with God, and that involves a decision. Gas station attendant, preacher, waitress, wife at home, executive at the office. You name it, and they all are faced with the same issue: We either make the time or it doesn't happen.

If I want to live with spiritual abundance, *I must find the time.*

Listening to God's Voice

ALBERT SCHWEITZER, ALSATIAN THEOLOGIAN, MUSICIAN, MEDICAL MISSIONARY (1875–1965)

You know of the disease in Central Africa called sleeping sickness . . . There also exists a sleeping sickness of the soul. Its most dangerous aspect is that one is unaware of its coming. That is why you have to be care-

ful. As soon as you notice the slightest sign of indifference, the moment you become aware of the loss of a certain seriousness, of longing, of enthusiasm and zest,
take it as a warning. You should realize that your soul
suffers if you live superficially. People need times in
which to concentrate, when they can search for their
innermost selves. It is tragic that most men have not
achieved this feeling of self-awareness. And finally, when
they hear the inner voice, they do not want to listen any-
more. They carry on as before so as not to be constantly
reminded of what they have lost. But as for you, resolve
to keep a quiet time both in your homes and here within
these peaceful walls when the bells ring on Sundays.
Then your souls can speak to you without being
drowned out by the hustle and bustle of everyday life.

FROM *THE SEARCH FOR MEANING,*
BY PHILIP L. BERMAN, EPIGRAPH

The Appearance and Disappearance of the Soul

JACOB NEEDLEMAN, AMERICAN PHILOSOPHER

A hundred, a thousand times a day, perhaps, "The
soul is aborted." An individual is completely unaware of
this loss and remains so throughout his whole life.
Without the necessary help and guidance, he never
reaches the orientation necessary for enabling these
everyday experiences to accumulate.

"Lost Christianity" is the lost or forgotten power of man to extract the pure energy of the soul from the experiences that make up his life. This possibility is distinct only in the most vivid or painful moments of our ordinary lives, but it can be discovered in all experiences if one knows how to seek it. Certain powerful experiences—such as the encounter with death or deep disappointment—are accompanied by the sensation of presence; an attention appears that is simultaneously open to higher, freer mind ("Spirit") and to all the perceptions, sensations, and emotions that constitute our ordinary self. One feels both separate and engaged in a new and entirely extraordinary way. One experiences "I Am." This is the soul (in inception).

It was a disaster for Christianity, according to Father Sylvan, when it adopted the notion that the soul of man already exists in finished form within human nature. This assumption about the given existence of the soul led to our identification of ordinary kinds of thoughts, emotions, and sensations with the soul, the higher part of ourselves, and hence to the futile and mistaken effort to perfect our being by perfecting our thoughts, emotions, or sensations, that is, the futile effort of thought to alter emotion or vice versa. The Christian teaching, as Father Sylvan presents it, says on the contrary that these psychological functions are incapable of altering each other. Change, transformation, can come only through the action of an objectively higher force: the Spirit. And this Spirit cannot find channels of action unless there exists something in man that can receive it and pass it on to all the parts of himself.

FROM *LOST CHRISTIANITY*, PP. 175–76.

And how is the disaster averted? By taking the time to come into the presence of God to pray. A door is opened. The Holy Spirit floods into our lives and brings the needed change. Jacob Needleman wants us to see that most of the society around us has made a serious error, thinking that improving one's outlook will eventually result in personal transformation. It doesn't work that way.

True recovery of spiritual abundance is always the result of the Holy Spirit's work in us. Keep working on improving yourself because that's worthwhile, but *don't make the mistake of assuming that self-improvement is the same thing as spiritual abundance.* Only God can give us this wonderful vitality.

In this age of counseling, we have to periodically stop and recognize that no counselor, therapist, teacher, guru, or whatever can transform our lives. The best that they can do is to help us get in touch with our inconsistencies and incongruencies. God is the only one who can alter us at the most fundamental level of our existence.

———————◆———————

Soul: Possession of
FULTON J. SHEEN

The possession of a soul means the undisturbed mastery of oneself, which is the secret of inner peace, as distinguished from a thousand agitations which make it fearful, unhappy, and disappointed. Only when the soul is possessed can anything else be enjoyed.[1]

FROM *LIFE OF CHRIST*, P. 50

———————◆———————

Through these passages, I was beginning to see that part of the reason that I felt like I had lost my soul was that I never was in control of this vital portion of my existence. Even with a Christian commitment, I was running around in a thousand directions at the same time, like a car falling apart while it is speeding down the highway. I let other people run my life, tell me what to do, how to do it. And I kept the broken car on the road by pushing down the truly important issues when they popped up.

When I looked around me, I realized that I was surrounded by thousands of people who had given possession of their lives over to something or someone else. It wasn't that they were bad or ineffective people; they had simply run out of all vitality. These folks were spiritually empty. They had given up spiritual control of their existence—and didn't even have a clue about what had occurred.

During my childhood, one of the few people who touched me spiritually was a man who came into our house every week through our television. He always walked in with a cape, wearing a small cap that looked like a Jewish prayer kepi. His pointed, dramatic talks held me spellbound.

In time, I learned that Bishop Fulton J. Sheen was one of the most powerful preachers in America. As an adult, I had the opportunity to meet and be with this man of profound spiritual intellect. I continued to listen when he spoke.

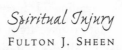

Spiritual Injury
FULTON J. SHEEN

But the power to do harm would never affect the souls of the apostles. The body can be injured without the consent of the soul, but the soul cannot be injured without its own consent. The only thing to be feared is losing, not human life, but the Divine life which is God.[2]

FROM *LIFE OF CHRIST*, P. 106

Soul: Fearing Those Who Can Kill

FULTON J. SHEEN

When He said: "I have conquered the world," He did not mean His followers would be immune from woes, pain, sorrow, and crucifixion. He gave no peace which promised a banishment from strife; for God hates peace in those destined for war. If the heavenly Father did not spare His Son, He, the heavenly Son, would not spare His disciples. What the Resurrection offered was not immunity from evil in the physical world, but immunity from sin in the soul.[3]

FROM *LIFE OF CHRIST*, P. 438

I started out discovering that my life was filled with "form replacing substance." After I worked my way through these readings, I discovered that once again it was possible to have form with substance. Put simply, I could find the reality of God in my church again. I could pray and make contact. The issue wasn't so difficult once I made the time to pursue my relationship with the Holy Spirit. Spiritual abundance awaited me there in that sacred space. Was making the time worthwhile? You bet!

PART THREE

* * *

Recovery:

Reclaiming

Our Spirituality

TWELVE

Finding Greater Spirituality: An Exercise

$\mathcal{W}$e have read the Scripture, studied the Church Fathers, and listened to the saints. Their experiences offer to us extraordinary insight and encouragement. After allowing their advice and direction to sink in, I found that I needed to settle into my own hermitages and move further from *knowing about* to *knowing*. All the material in countless books does little good unless the insight is put into practice. I found that at this point I must take the solitary journey with no other companion than the resurrected Christ beckoning me to follow Him. I believe that He wants you to join us.

In my spiritual travels, I found particular road signs and special paths were significant. I offer these discoveries to you as primers for your pump.

Do Not Fear the Silence

A distraught, depressed pastor once came to the psychiatrist Carl Jung for counsel. Jung asked about the man's employment demands. He proudly reported a consistent sixty-hour-a-week work schedule. Jung's prescription was for the man to go home at 5:00 P.M. each day and spend the next three hours in complete solitude, doing absolutely nothing.

The pastor returned in a week with a report of significant relief. He reported happily, "I've been able to read a number of books I had missed."

Jung retorted, "I told you to do *nothing.*" The minister was shocked and explained he couldn't possibly do *nothing* but be alone with himself.

With a wry smile Jung answered, "And you visit *that* on people sixty hours a week?"

Are we really any different? We hit the house and the stereo goes on, the TV is added, and we hope for a phone call. Like the pastor, we fear the shape of absolute silence.

Remember this: no silence, no spirituality.

I found that quietness was a vital element in growing in my relationship with Christ. However, the problem of the availability of stillness almost seemed to create another endangered species. In Henri Nouwen's *The Way of the Heart,* his discussion

of the desert spirituality of the Church Fathers
warns us about the difficulty of silence today.

> One of our main problems is that in this chatty
> society, silence has become a fearful thing. For most
> people, silence creates itchiness and nervousness.
> Many experience stillness not as full and rich, but as
> empty and hollow. Silence is like a gaping abyss
> which can swallow them. As soon as the minister
> suggests during a worship service, "Let us be silent
> for a few moments," people tend to become restless
> and preoccupied with only one thought: *When will
> this be over?* Imposed silence often creates hostility
> and resentment. Many ministers who have experi-
> mented with silence in their services have soon
> found out that silence can be more difficult than
> divine and have quickly picked up the signals that
> the congregation is saying: "Please keep talking."[1]

No, the task is not easy . . . but it is still essential.
After repeated attempts to get completely quiet, I
began to discover a placid place at the center of my
being. Before I found the tranquil terrain of my
inner self, my prayers were words flung toward the
ceiling, desperately hoping some expression got
beyond the roof. After I located this space, I knew I
had located the point of spiritual connection. Frantic, pleading words were no longer necessary. The

Spirit began to intercede with "groanings and long-ings" beyond words.

I suggest you start by setting aside five minutes when you do nothing but wait in silence. If nothing else, you will find this exercise to be a marvelous help in remembering everything you should have done earlier. Thoughts and hints of activities will float from all directions. No problem. This interference is par for the course. Simply keep a pad, write down the intrusions, and dismiss the thoughts. However, keep on and don't let the unexpected derail the train. The next step is to sit quietly for ten minutes, fifteen minutes, and finally push it up to thirty. Persevere and expand your capacity to sit silently.

I quickly found that placing a pad and pencil on the desk was vital. As each reminder came up, I simply wrote the task down and dismissed it from my mind. I didn't have to worry about forgetting, and my mind could be at ease. Like a glass of muddy water settling, distractions drifted to the bottom and clarity returned. A number of sessions were required before I got the hang of getting completely quiet.

The goal is not to perform a technique of medi-tation, but rather to get ready to enter the presence of God. The Bible says we are to love the Lord our God with our whole heart, mind, and soul. I found that most of the time I approached God with a will-ing heart, half a mind, and no soul. The exercise in quietness remedies the problem. The task is to get all barriers out of the way.

Perhaps a different perspective on silence will encourage you. Metropolitan Anthony wrote:

> We have to learn to distinguish two sorts of silence: God's silence and our own inner silence. First the silence of God, often harder to bear than His refusal . . . Second, the silence of man, deeper than speech, in closer communion with God than any words.
>
> God's silence to our prayers can last only a short time, or it may seem to go on forever. Christ was silent to the prayers of the Canaanite woman, and this led her to gather up all her faith and hope and human love to offer to God so that He might extend the conditions of the kingdom beyond the chosen people. The silence of Christ provoked her to respond, to grow to her capacity. And God may do the same to us with shorter or longer silences—to summon our strength and faithfulness and lead us to deeper relationship with Him than [would have been] possible had it been easy.[2]

Only after you become comfortable with the silence are you prepared to go on. If you are seriously reading this book and chapter as a guide to finding your spirituality, I would suggest you stop at this point and read no further until you have been able to stay in silence for thirty minutes. More knowledge won't help. Only experience will profit you.

MEETING JESUS

Once we are settled in silence, our task is to meet Jesus, the resurrected Lord. The quest is not a learning experience as much as an encounter with God. The objective is to rejuvenate the soul so we will be able to recognize the real person as it happens.

Learning to pray "The Jesus Prayer" proved to be an important turning point in my quest for renewed spiritual vitality. I discovered a new sense of where to look in my desire to find the life of God.

Reflections on The Jesus Prayer, by a nameless priest of the Byzantine church, tells us:

> God is present *within* us; He manifests Himself in *ourselves;* this inner manifestation of God is all important; there is no religious life, no life of the Spirit without this; our sanctification and our salvation hinge on this. Moreover, this manifestation of God in us depends on ourselves; it takes place only if we want it to take place.[3]

During my sojourn in the Benedictine monastery, I learned the value of The Jesus Prayer to help the process. For two thousand years, Christians have dwelt in the presence of their Lord by simply praying over and over the name *Jesus*.

We are not experimenting with some form of Oriental meditation or looking for mystical moments. In contrast, we are simply doing what lovers do when they gaze into each other's eyes and find no other words adequately express the heart except the other's name. The goal is not petition or intercession but simply affirmation in love.

Often The Jesus Prayer is expanded into a longer form. We repeat the prayer of the blind man on the road to Jericho, "Lord Jesus Christ, Son of God, have mercy on me, a sinner." Each word is repeated slowly as we ponder the message while praying the meaning. For example:

Lord: "Jesus, You are the Lord of my life. Thank you for remembering me."

Jesus: "You are God's gift to us. You died for me."

Christ: "You are my Messiah, the One who will lead me to all fulfillment."

Son: "You were truly a human being. You know what my life is about."

of God: "You take me to the Father. You are the Way, the Truth, the Life."

Have mercy: "Please overlook my inadequacies as I name them."

on me: "I rejoice that I am important to You."
a sinner: "My life would be completely empty, guilty, and hope less without Your love."

The Byzantine priest reminds us:

The Jesus Prayer does not end with the word *sinner* for the simple reason that The Jesus Prayer does not end at all. *Sinner* is the last word of our exhalation. It empties our lungs. And as we begin to fill them again with our next breath, the heartbeat, starting with the word *Lord,* begins to beat out the Good News once more. As in a musical rhythm, the last weak beat in the measure serves as the springboard to the strong first beat of the next measure. *Sinner* is the weak beat that leads us to *Lord,* and the Lord is our strong beat. And so the dance goes on.[4]

I found that as I prayed and considered each aspect of this prayer over and over again, my sense of presence grew. Equally important for the journey, I began to have a deepening awareness of my own spirituality, the God capacity within me. Something long neglected and overlooked was again taking form. Like a weight lifter building atrophied muscles, new form and shape began to emerge.

What happens during these moments of inner dialogue? The priest of the Byzantine church says:

The eternal Word of God took a body of the Blessed Virgin, died and rose gloriously on the Third Day in that same divinized body. And, because by baptism I became one with that body, and because by Holy Communion I am constantly sustaining that bodily oneness with Christ and growing in it—for these reasons, when I bring my mind down into my heart and listen, I discern not just my own heartbeat, but also Christ's. It is because my body is Christ's body that I am a Temple. And my heart (His heart) is the innermost sanctuary of that Temple. Therefore, when my mind is in my heart—and not only my mind, but my animal and vegetative drives and energies, too—then I am truly at prayer. For prayer is nothing else than attentiveness to God's presence. God is with us. "Let us be attentive," as we say in the Divine Liturgy.[5]

In this sense, we are not praying as much as learning to pray, because only the Holy Spirit can really teach us how to commune with God. At each step we take forward into our own spirituality, the hand of Jesus meets us and takes us onward. We think we are doing the work only to discover that the divine source of instruction stands behind us prior to any effort on our part. We do not discover our spirituality as much as we have that spirituality revealed to us.

The unknown author of the spiritual classic *The Cloud of Unknowing*, written around the year 1375, put it this way, "He kindled your desire for Himself, and bound you to Him by the chain of such longing."[6] Thomas Merton said it differently: "True contemplation is not a psychological trick but a theological grace. It can come to us only as a gift."[7]

REMOVING THE BLOCKS AND BARRIERS

Getting spirituality into view is only the start. We must not mistake a glimpse as being the equivalent of fullness. Henri Nouwen tells us:

> When Anthony heard the word of Jesus, "Go and sell what you own and give the money to the poor . . . then come and follow me," he took it as a call to escape from the compulsions of the world. He moved away from his family, lived in poverty in a hut on the edge of his village, and occupied himself with manual work and prayer. But soon he realized that more was required of him. He had to face his enemies—anger and greed—head-on and let himself be totally transformed into a new being. His old, false self had to die and a new self had to be born. For this Anthony withdrew into the complete solitude of the desert.
>
> Solitude is the furnace of transformation. With-

out solitude we remain victims of our society and continue to be entangled in the illusions of the false self. Jesus Himself entered into this furnace.[8]

We do well to note that the Eastern Orthodox Church, which puts great emphasis on the spiritual life, doesn't offer much guidance on prayer techniques. In contrast, prayer manuals are filled with direction on one's moral posture and the necessary spiritual conditions for effective praying. *Getting it right* is more important than *doing it right.*

Once we begin to develop a sense of inner space and living prayer, we will become aware of more serious barriers than simple everyday distractions. Our spirituality is often calloused, encased, and encrusted with a protective shell. Often considerable time is required to become aware of the barricades that years of painful experience have erected within us. We may not be aware that we are our own worst enemies.

Once we begin to tear away the false self, we will not find that the path is automatically easier. To the contrary, we will find ourselves in another form of spiritual warfare. We have to struggle with formerly nonthreatening demons that cohabited with us. Now the house must be cleaned and the intruders cast out. Abba Elias, one of the Desert Fathers, reminds us of where our strength must be found for this battle in the desert of our own souls.

An old man was living in a temple and the demons came to say to him, "Leave this place which belongs to us," and the old man said, "No place belongs to you." Then they began to scatter his palm leaves about, one by one, and the old man went on gathering them together with persistence. A little later the devil took his hand and pulled him to the door. When the old man reached the door, he seized the lintel with the other hand, crying out, "Jesus, save me." Immediately the devil fled away. Then the old man began to weep. Then the Lord said to him, "Why are you weeping?" and the old man said, "Because the devils have dared to seize a man and treat him like this." The Lord said to him, "You had been careless. As soon as you turned to me again, you see I was beside you."[9]

Each of us must be prepared for the battle to take many forms as we push on to fully recover our spirituality. We must remember that the one we seek is already there waiting to help us get through the blockades and the mine fields secretly set to stop us. In the silence and solitude, we must fervently seek the intervention of Christ to accomplish for us what we cannot achieve for ourselves.

HEARING HIS VOICE

In the beginning, God spoke and everything came into existence. Then, in 4 B.C. God spoke again and the Word became flesh. The Creator is a God who communicates, and the recovery of our spirituality is the restoration of our ability to hear. Finding our souls is more than developing awareness. We are called on to a relationship analogous to what Adam and Eve knew in the Garden.

You can develop the capacity to hear your heavenly Father speak your name.

Your spirituality is the place of reception. David Watson put the promise in these terms: "God did not finish speaking to us when the Scriptures were com-pleted . . . God is the living God, the God of today; and every day He wants us to enjoy a living relation-ship with Him, involving a two-way conversation."[10]

After weeks of exploring silence and praying The Jesus Prayer, I reached the level where I was praying for an hour a day in silent contemplation. The expe-rience was rich, rewarding, and reconstituting. Then one day, I realized I had reached a new plateau. Something more was just on the other side of that single hour.

At the end of one of these periods, the story of the boy Samuel and his calling from God came to mind. I remember Samuel wasn't clear about how God spoke. The old high priest Eli told the boy to respond at his next visitation, "Speak Lord, for Your servant hears." With that phrase ringing in my mind, at the end of the next hour of silent prayer, I said the same words aloud. Much to my surprise, I found my mind was filled with a new vivid dialogue.

Like a stream of consciousness, a flow of verbal direction ran through my thinking. I immediately grabbed my pencil and wrote furiously. Trying to keep from censoring myself, I simply let come what may. Eventually the words ebbed away in my thinking, and I had a page full of notes.

In the following days, I eagerly pursued my new-found discipline. The flow of material increased, as did my capacity to hear the voice of God. In addition, I found the direction I received was extremely helpful in making decisions and knowing the will of God. Often the communiqués had messages or insights for other people. Sometimes Jesus seemed to speak as a friend. At other times, the voice seemed to be more clearly like the gentle moving of the Holy Spirit. On occasion, the majestic voice of the Father broke through. There was no question in my mind that I had found a new and profound sense of connecting with the Holy Spirit.

Slowly, I began to evolve a new sense of how spiritual communication works. As the mind has an intuitive function, the soul has a unique sense of knowing. The more I reflected on how intuition operates, the more clear I became about my spiritual experiences.

The mind can calculate like an adding machine compiles numbers and then comes to a total, a conclusion. We call this capacity "syllogistic logic." Conclusions are drawn from the sum total of our experiences. On the other hand, intuition bubbles up with a logic born out of our inner knowing. Insight offers us answers without reference to the system of compilation. We intuitively know when our children are lying or when something bad is about to happen. A message comes out of the wild blue yonder and flashes through our minds. We *know* that we know.

The more I paid attention to my intuitions, the more I was aware of how often God speaks. While inspiration is not rational or irrational, it is often beyond syllogistic logic and arises, as does insight, from our inner core. We must learn neither to ignore nor to censor what bubbles up from the inner aquifers. We simply listen. In the beginning, the important thing is just to clear out the wellsprings for a continuous flow of inspiration.

As my collection of notes piled up, I realized that a considerable amount of material was accumulating. Some of the recordings seemed mediocre; others seemed to contain highly significant direction too important to be lost. I recognized a need to systematize my most helpful discoveries and began transferring this data into a journal.

The journal was arranged with three sections. In the first of the notebook, I kept my discoveries about prayer. I kept insights into how to pray and be spiritually aware by date. Writing Hebrew style, I recorded the promises of the Holy Spirit in the back of the book, going in the opposite direction from the usual front to back order. I dated each indication of direction.

Possibly the most important section of the journal was in the middle. When I heard wrong or the promises turned out to be erroneous, I recorded my error. Periodically, I would go back and try to sort out why I heard wrong. Quickly, I found the miscommunications offered very important insight into my spirituality as well.

FINE-TUNING THE INNER EAR

Being in touch with the soul doesn't make us automatically right or every intuitive nudge correct. In fact, with time I discovered hearing God accurately, consistently, and with understanding was much more complex than I thought in the early euphoric days of spiritual breakthrough. For example, often there is considerable contamination as personal desires sweep in and pollute the message.

If the moral climate isn't right, the message can be distorted like sounds fading when batteries are going dead on a dictation device. We do well to be highly suspicious of ourselves.

How do we avoid such pitfalls? The discipline of

journaling is a necessity. We have to pay the price of hours spent in intercession, meditation, and silence to learn the pathways through our soul. Possibly you want to say back to me that you don't have time to do this amount of soul inquiry. Let me ask you in return, do you *actually* have time for anything else . . . lest you gain the world and lose your soul?

As I began training people to use this technique and listen to God, I discovered that many sincere people confuse their thoughts with inspiration. Whatever blipped through their minds during prayer was assumed to be holy. They might start speaking a prayer message aloud to a group of listeners, but their revelation was only a stream of consciousness that was nothing more than talking to themselves with their eyes closed. Some times these "messages" were destructive and misleading to people.

I quickly came to see that we needed to have clear guidelines to test what was coming from our spirituality. Here are some time-tried directions for clear reception and understanding the voice of God accurately. They will help you stay on track as you pursue the depths of what the Holy Spirit wants to tell you.

UNDERSTANDING THE VOICE OF GOD

Does the message agree with Scripture?

God speaks with one voice, and the centuries

don't change the message. Healthy people will keep referencing biblical guidelines. Compromise on this front is deadly. The better that you know the Bible, the more clearly you will hear God speak.

Does the message find resonance with other spiritual people?

We need spiritual companions in this walk. A spiritual director is a must. Sharing the inner movements of the soul helps establish a vital objectivity that distances us from the false self. If we are uncomfortable sharing some aspect of the message with a confidential friend, we have a strong clue that something is wrong.

Does it stand the test of time?

God is consistent with Himself, and subsequently truth is one of the best indicators of what He is saying. Like the sun coming up, the truth will get brighter with the passing of time. Check your journal periodically to see if verifications are there.

Is the emotional tone spiritually significant?

Often people are told, "You will know the will of God because of the peace you receive." Such advice is only a half-truth! In many instances, the Holy Spirit challenges, corrects, and *doesn't make us happy*. As a matter of fact, I am suspicious of inspiration that only confirms my prejudgments. When a contrary or surprising emotion appears, I take the uncomfortable feeling very seriously.

What fruit does this spiritual encounter produce?

Am I becoming more gentle, loving, thoughtful, preserving? Is the work of the kingdom of God being accomplished through my spiritual discoveries? If the answers aren't positive to myself and to others, I need to take a second look.

Do we need a competent therapist or counselor for some issues?

The emphasis is on *competence*. Wounds from childhood and traumas along the way seriously damage many of us and make it much more difficult to get in touch with the Holy Spirit. These same conflicts distort inspiration. Therapy may be necessary to make sure that we have our head on straight.

These guidelines will help you tune out static and distortion. And remember, the more you listen, the greater will become your awareness of your soul.

FINDING A COMPANION
FOR THE JOURNEY

Prolonged time working with our spirituality often reveals we have significant issues that need someone else's insight to keep matters in perspective.

Possibly we need spiritual healing. Often, we must find spiritual companions trained as doctors of the soul. A competent spiritual director with the capacity to be a soulmate is a rare and invaluable friend. His or her insights become like a compass for a sailor.

Long a discipline in the Roman Catholic, Orthodox, and Anglican traditions, spiritual directors are trained to blend Scripture, psychology, and theology into the art of restoring and ordering spirituality. Expert listeners, spiritual directors probe our inner world with us, removing emotional shrapnel and splinters from bad memories, and unmasking the blind spots in our perceptions of ourselves. They help us sort out confusion and shame so that the secret self can emerge and be examined.

In the long haul, a spiritual director is essential to test what we believe the Holy Spirit is saying. Self-deception is an inevitable part of every life. A straightforward spiritual friend who is unafraid to tell us the truth will keep us from the seductiveness of our own dreams and the nonsense of our fantasies. This person will help guide us out of trouble.

Today, confusion abounds! A few decades ago, no one dared to baptize an opinion by saying, "The Lord told me." Today, every impulse and whim of the faithful is claimed to be completely God-breathed. Rather than saying, "I am moving to another church because I like the other place better," everyone is now "led to a new ministry." Many Christians would be saved considerable embarrassment by having a spiritual director help them sort out the baloney from the blessing.

If nothing else, a spiritual guide will help us maintain the disciplines necessary for consistent living and keeping our spirituality in balance.

FINDING OUR WAY HOME

What does it mean to have found your spirituality? To hear the voice of God? Not as an idea but as an inner reality? Not only is God-consciousness recovered, but a profound sense of relationship with the ultimate Lover of our life follows.

> This is the nature of the encounter, not that I am stumbling towards the Abba Father, but that the Abba Father is running towards me. It is not that I love God but that God believes in me. The discovery at the heart of contemplation is not that I am contemplating the divine love, but that the divine love is contemplating me. He sees me and understands and accepts me, He has compassion on me, He creates me afresh from moment to moment, and He protects me and is with me through death and into life beyond.[11]

I know of nothing that encourages and touches me more than to realize that in my feeble moments of turning my attention to the Father, He has already been waiting there a long time for me to wake up and pay attention to the invisible hand on my shoulder. My discovery has been that His grace is always greater than my sin, His love more ready than my call of repentance and questing after forgiveness. My desire for a deeper and broader spirituality grows every time that I realize the awesomeness of His overwhelming love.

THIRTEEN

Living the Abundance

The renowned philosopher Arthur Schopenhauer was walking obliviously down the street, in deep thought, when he accidentally ran into a stranger. Schopenhauer's seeming indifference caused the other man to shake his fist and shout angrily, "Just who do you think you are?"

The dismayed thinker looked at the upset pedestrian and replied in consternation, "Who am I? How I wish I knew!"

Even if apocryphal, the incident is a good parable of our time. Leonard Bernstein observed, "Half the people are drowned, and the other half are swimming in the wrong direction."[1] Even though decades ago, T. S. Eliot warned us about becoming hollow people with straw-stuffed heads, we are often gleefully unaware of our deadly predicament. Technology saves us from confrontation with harsh reality by offering an infinite number of new toys each year that keep us from recognizing our aimless meandering trek from birth to the grave. No time left to think while the menu options of the Internet are popping up before our eyes. Just push the buttons and bring up the endless choices! Are these diversions any different from offering lollipops to an upset child as a distraction from the pain?

In *The Sane Society*, psychologist Erich Fromm gave us the bottom line: "In the nineteenth century the problem was that God is dead; in the twentieth century the problem is that man is dead."[2] And what will it be in the twenty-first century? The world is dead?

THE HOPE OF THE FAITHFUL

The answer is not religion *per se*. Unfortunately, spiritually dead churches have often promised peace at any price, offering sterile placebos for cancer of the soul. Emotional tranquility is the prize regardless of what must be denied or pushed out of view. God is seen as a celestial Tylenol painkiller to be taken every morning and night until we no longer feel what we know is true.

An unknown author wrote, "For some people, religion is like an artificial limb. It has neither warmth nor life; and although it helps them to stumble along, it never becomes part of them. It must be strapped on each day."[3]

A new phenomenon of the current day is self-invented, do-it-yourself religions that use Christian language but have no connection to the Church or its past. Often called New Age, these groups talk about spirituality but can't offer transcendence. They wade into the marketplace, selling emotional well-being by teaching people how to think more positively or to rely on psychic powers. However, in this context, prayer is essentially nothing more than talking to oneself. Talk of spirituality is more on the level of Ray Charles belting out inner agony. The New Agers, too, are specialists in crutches, artificial legs, and plastic arms.

Our hope lies in the recovery of the abundance that is ours through a *daily relationship with the God of Israel, our heavenly Father*. Through Jesus Christ, He has opened a new door for us to walk through.

The four Gospels demand that we stop in our tracks, turn around, and start traveling toward God. During the journey, our spirituality will be restored. In a few sweeping sentences, Jesus taught us what it means to give up mindless distractions as well as our quixotic quest for fame, fortune, and significance in order to become whole:

"Therefore I tell you, do not be anxious about your life, what you shall eat or what you shall drink,

227

nor about your body, what you shall put on . . . And which of you by being anxious can add one cubit to his span of life? . . . But seek first his kingdom and his righteousness, and all these things shall be yours as well." (Matt. 6:25, 27, 33 RSV)

Jesus taught that life in the kingdom restores the soul and our identity.

The framers of the Westminster Catechism had this objective when they suggested that the purpose of life is to know and enjoy God forever. The point of our existence is not to do or accomplish any particular thing. Rather, *the restoration of spiritual relationship is the singular most significant achievement of anyone's lifetime.*

OUR COMMON DESTINY

From the beginning of this book, we have been faced with a problem. We are looking for something no one has ever seen with his or her eyes. Jesus had the same difficulty in calling people to life. In Carson McCullers's novel *The Heart Is a Lonely Hunter,* a teenager tries to explain to a deaf mute how music sounds. With frantic gestures, the girl stands in front of poor Mr. Singer trying to get him to read her lips. Eventually she realizes how hopeless her attempts are. One can't explain color to the blind or sound to the deaf—or life to the dead. Our task in the previous pages has not been easier.

And yet we have seen a multitude of witnesses from across the centuries point the way. They told us the soul is not a place as much as a capacity. As important as the reestablishment of contact is, the real objective is a life of continuous dialogue.

Few people understood living through their spirituality as well as did the Quaker theologian Thomas R. Kelly:

> Deep within us all there is an amazing inner sanctuary of the soul, a holy place, a Divine Center, a speaking Voice, to which we may continuously return. Eternity is at our hearts, pressing upon our time-torn lives, warming us with intimations of an astounding destiny, calling us home unto Itself. Yielding to these persuasions, gladly committing ourselves in body and soul, utterly and completely, to the Light Within which illumines the face of God and casts new shadows and new glories upon the face of men. It is a seed stirring to life if we do not choke it. It is the Shekinah of the soul, the Presence in the midst. Here is the Slumbering Christ, stirring to be awakened, to become the soul we clothe in earthly form and action.[4]

Our task is to keep one foot in the world of bills,

babies, and doorbells while keeping the other in the hidden place of eternity. Our vision must constantly shift back and forth from this realm of artificial lightbulbs to the place where the glorious light of God alone shines. Once we've found focus, we must make sure our visits are far more than seasonal or prompted by the pressure of problems or personal tragedy. Destiny is not "doing something" but living there.

THE ANSWER

Once the Holy Spirit restores our contact with God, we discover that the risen Christ calls us by name as surely as He summoned Mary Magdalene on the first Easter morning. Individual and unique ways of hearing the gentle calling of God become very important. Our task is to live at the place where the voice arises.

The objective of our spiritual quest is not to collect right ideas, perfect our theology, find ecstatic religious experiences, seek the latest avant-garde fad, or even learn new rules to live by. *The goal is to live out of our soul minute by minute, hour by hour, day by day*.

John Woolman, a Quaker tailor, attempted to arrange every aspect of his private and business life so that nothing could crowd out his continuous inner experience with Christ. As he worked from the altar of his soul, Woolman was also increasingly aware of the evils of his day: slave trading, usury, and the Indian wars.

Thomas R. Kelly described the practice of believers like Woolman in these terms:

> There is a way of ordering our mental life on more than one level at once. On one level we may be thinking, discussing, seeing, calculating, meeting all the demands of external affairs. But deep within, behind the scenes, at a profounder level, we may also be in prayer and adoration, song and worship and a gentle receptiveness to divine breathings.[5]

Kelly believed that living spiritually means constantly bringing all the affairs of life into the presence of God and rethinking each event in the light of Christ before bringing it back into the world of daily events. He said perceptively, "Facts remain facts, when brought into the Presence in the deeper level, but their value, their significance, is wholly realigned."[6] What might we call this process? I think *spiritual abundance* will do fine.

Living from the soul is quite practical. Henry Blackaby and Claude King described the straightforward nature of spiritually-alive life in their book, *Experiencing God*. I believe that you will find that these words help put your life back on track and keep you in tune with the heavenly Father's divine purposes.

God is absolutely trustworthy. You can trust Him to guide you and provide for you. Remember: "It is God who works in you both to will and to do for His good pleasure" (Phil. 2:13). Would you consider doing the following?

- Agree with God that you will follow Him one day at a time.
- Agree to follow Him even when He does not spell out all the details.
- Agree that you will let Him be your Way.

Now consider praying this prayer: "Lord, I will do anything that Your kingdom requires of me. Wherever You want me to be, I'll go. Whatever the circumstances, I'm willing to follow. If You want to meet a need through my life, I am Your servant; and I will do whatever is required."[7]

The last chapter offered encouragement to develop the discipline of listening as you quietly wait at your personal "silent center." Sacred history demonstrates that the Holy Spirit communicates with us in many ways. For many, the Scripture is the place of direct communication with God. The more time spent in the Word, the clearer the directives become. Other Christians find holy Communion is their primary means of encounter. Wine and bread are visible signs of an invisible spiritual transaction. As food nourishes the body, the sacrament feeds the soul.

Quakers sit in silence and wait. The Orthodox use icons—holy pictures—to experience God. Pentecostals speak in tongues and listen for prophecies and exhortations to find God. Christians have used a wide range of prayer methods to help believers dwell in the place of the inner light. The most important issue is that we *live in this* place of encounter.

Forget the e-mail, the fax, and the latest upgrade for your modem for a while. Let spiritual communication rebuild your life through eternal communiqués.

THE CLOISTER OF THE HEART

Because Jesus Christ is the same yesterday, today, and forever, He alone is the final guide and goal. Far from a figure in the past, the risen Christ stands on the other side of silence, waiting to restore us to Himself.

Many church people are surprised to hear that communication is reciprocal. They hope their intercessions will get beyond the roof but know nothing of anything coming back down. Because contemporary

233

Christians tend toward a "fast, good" approach to prayer, spiritual malnutrition is rampant. We grab a little something to keep us going as we hurry on to the next event in our lives.

Only by living in our personal quiet center can we learn to listen. Through contemplation we learn to let the speech of God come up from within. Thomas R. Kelly understood this deeper level well:

> There is no new technique for entrance upon this stage where the soul in its deeper levels is continuously at home in Him. The processes of inward prayer do not grow more complex, but more simple. In the early weeks we begin with simple, whispered words. Formulate them spontaneously, "Thine only. Thine only." Or seize upon a fragment of the Psalms: "so panteth my soul after Thee, O God." Repeat them inwardly, over and over again, for the conscious cooperation of the surface level is needed at first, before prayer sinks into the second level as habitual divine orientation. Change the phrases, as you feel led, from hour to hour or from forenoon to afternoon. If you wander, return and begin again. But the time will come when verbalization is not so imperative, and yields place to the attitudes of soul which you meant the words to express, attitudes of humble bowing before Him, attitudes of lifting high your whole being before Him that the Light may

shine into the last crevice and drive away all darkness, attitudes of approach and nestling in the cover of His wings, attitudes of amazement and marvel at His transcendent glory, attitudes of self-abandonment, attitudes of feeding in an inward Holy Supper upon the Bread of Life.[8]

Through the practice of such ways, we are filled with spiritual abundance.

THE CONDITIONS FOR ABIDING

Jesus said, "If anyone loves Me, he will keep My word; and My Father will love him, and We will come to him and make Our home with him" (John 14:23). The critical principle for living spiritually is *obedience*. We need not be theologians, mystics, prophets, or hermits to abide constantly at the center. The old hymn was clear: "Trust and obey, for there's no other way to be happy." Saint Augustine offered the simple principle, *credo un intelligum*, "I believe and therefore I know," reversing the usual procedure by which people determine what is true— through empirical evidence. Through obedience, we authenticate and verify the truth of our faith. Only by living out what we believe day by day, year by year, do we come to know in time that our convictions are more real than the tangible world around us.

Simple faithfulness is a form of living out of the soul. Like the use of memory or retaining muscle tone, use is critical to maintenance. Daily obedience is the equivalent of a trip to the gym to keep the body toned.

In *Experiencing God*, obedience is described as our moment of truth. In many ways, obedience is your moment of truth. What you *do* will:

1. Reveal what you believe about Him.
2. Determine whether you will experience His mighty work in you and through you.
3. Determine whether you will come to know Him more intimately. [9]

Henry Blackaby said, "Whenever you sense that obedience is too costly, it indicates that you have misunderstood who you are and what you have."[10]

Like trust in a marriage relationship, faithfulness is essential if we are to live our spirituality with the One who is the lover of our lives. Fidelity is the secret of spiritual knowledge.

THE SHAPE OF ETERNITY IN US

We can put away the anatomy charts and X-ray machines. We cannot locate our spirituality with a stethoscope or electrodes. Poets and artists are better guides than anthropologists and scientists. The poor in spirit will get there much quicker than the brilliant and forceful. Rather than peering through a microscope, we do better to get down on our knees.

The longer we live in spiritual abundance, the more obvious will be the imprint of eternity on our lives. Irenaeus once said of Jesus the Christ's coming, "He became what we are that we might become who He is." Isn't that spiritual abundance? Our spiritual-ity is the real us, our essence, the fingerprint of God on our lives. Once renewed, our soul is both the cen-ter and circumference of our existence. We are filled with the Holy Spirit.

What might such life of spiritual abundance look like? Consider a concluding parable, the story of the Curé d'Ars.

As a young man, he was considered something of a dunce. He further embarrassed his parents by deciding to become a priest. In his first parish assign-ment, the vicar considered the recent seminarian too stupid to preach Sunday sermons. But when the bishop gave the devout young man his own parish, the young man offered his meager gifts completely to God. Rather than rely on scholarship, personality, or public relations skills, the priest completely gave himself to God in fervent daily prayer.

From his obscure post, the Curé's fame began to spread across France. Hundreds of thousands of people began making pilgrimages to Ars to sit at his feet and be blessed by the simple priest's teaching and preaching. When he would leave the church after a service, the press of the crowds was so great, it would take him thirty minutes to cross the small square in front of the church.

In 1925, sixty-six years after his death, the Curé d'Ars was canonized as the saint of parish priests. Because he gave of his humble gifts in faithful obedience, the Curé's spirituality was a marvel to behold.

Would the Curé d'Ars have been pleased at having been canonized if he'd known about the event? Probably he'd have been more embarrassed. What counted to him wasn't the recognition from others but the intimate, ongoing relationship with his heavenly Father. He had found the shape of eternity within himself long before his death.

Setting the Sail Again

I started the first chapter explaining how I had lost my spiritual bearings. A voyage across the sea called "life" had turned into a storm, and the result was a shipwreck. Too much *good* stuff had pushed the *best* out of the way, and the most important ingredients in my life had disappeared, lost under a pile of daily pressures. What can I tell you about where I am today?

I found that the recovery of spiritual abundance

brings surprises—one of them is that God often isn't nearly as concerned as we are about particular issues that seem quite pressing. Listening diligently to the Holy Spirit surprised me. At times when I was sure that I was marching down the right street, the voice of God told me I was in the wrong block. I found that He wasn't nearly as concerned with what I was doing *as who I was*. Identity remained the challenge.

During my adolescent years, I struggled a great deal with my identity. Having been adopted as a child, I labored to understand and know who my biological parents were. I wanted to know my father's name and was haunted by that empty space in my memory. I couldn't locate something that was basic, essential, and vital, and I felt diminished. Much to my surprise, the recovery of my spirituality filled that gap in a very unexpected way. To my surprise, I found out "who I was."

My father is the Father of the Lord Jesus Christ. Jesus called him "Abba" (which means Daddy or Poppa), and I found that I was supposed to do the same with my Creator. His touch filled my life with a sense of direction and purpose beyond anything that I thought possible, and now I understand that He continues to hold my life like a father holds his newborn child in his arms. And knowing *who I was* told me *what I was supposed to do*.

The heavenly Father is deeply concerned about

the human heart. He wants love to pump through our veins. And if we don't seem to have enough affection, He is more than willing to fill us when our natural capacity to love has run low. Jesus told us that the world would recognize that we are His disciples by how we love each other.

If spiritual abundance means anything, I have found that it is the recovery of the capacity to love . . . even people who have severely injured us.

Is it hard sometimes? Sure. Do we occasionally slip and do hateful things? Absolutely. But our boat is set in the water, going in the right direction, and at the end of the ride, we are at that place where our heavenly Father wants us to be. Sound good? Absolutely.

Can I recommend one thing for you to pursue this year? Put aside the secondary stuff and seek spiritual abundance. You will never be sorry that you did!

ENDNOTES

Chapter 1

1. Mary Caroline Richards, *Centering* (Middletown, Conn.: Wesleyan University Press, 1962), 33.

Chapter 3

1. From a graduation speech at Harvard University, 8 June 1978.

Chapter 4

1. Excerpt "Are Music and Movies Killing America's Soul?" © 1995 Time, Inc. Reprinted by permission.

2. Summary of "America, What's Gone Wrong?" by William Bennett (originally published in *The Virginian Pilot* and *The Ledger Star*, 24 April 1999, C1). Summary reprinted by permission from *Current Thoughts and Trends*, July 1999, 24.

Chapter 5

1. Excerpt from *The Spiritual Life of Children*. Copyright © 1990 by Robert Coles. Reprinted by permission of Houghton Mifflin Co. All rights reserved.

2. Excerpt from *Soul Food* by Sheila Ferguson, copyright © 1989 by Sheila Ferguson. Used by permission of Grove/Atlantic, Inc.

Chapter 6

1. Sam Keen, *Fire in the Belly* (New York: Bantam/Doubleday/Dell Publishers, 1992), 110–111.

2. Greil Marcus, *Mystery Train* (New York: Dutton, a division of Penguin USA, 1990), 32–36.

3. Elizabeth Burns, *The Late Liz* (New York: Meredith, 1957), 1.

4. Ibid., 342.

Chapter 7

1. William Styron, *Sophie's Choice* (New York: Bantam, 1979), 177.

2. Elie Wiesel, *Night* (New York: Bantam, 1960), 109.

3. From *The Hiding Place,* by Corrie ten Boom with John and Elizabeth Sherrill (Chappaqua, N.Y.: Chosen Books LLC, 1971), 198–199.

Chapter 11

1. Excerpt from *Life of Christ: Complete and Unabridged* (New York: Image Books, 1977), 50.

2. Ibid., 106.

3. Ibid., 438.

Chapter 12

1. Henri J. M. Nouwen, *The Way of the Heart* (New York: Seabury, 1981), 59.

2. Metropolitan Anthony et al., *Courage to Pray* (Crestwood, N.Y.: St. Vladimir's Seminary Press, 1997), 41. Used by permission.

3. Author unknown, *Reflections on the Jesus Prayer* (Denville, N.J.: Dimension, 1948), 21.

4. Ibid., 25.

5. Ibid.

6. Author unknown, *The Cloud of Unknowing,* 51.

7. Thomas Merton, *Contemplative Prayer* (New York: Image Books, 1971), 115.

8. Nouwen, *The Way of the Heart,* 25.

9. Benedicta Ward, trans. *The Sayings of the Desert Fathers* (London: Mowbrays, 1975), 69.

10. David Watson, *Discipleship* (Hodder & Stoughton, 1981), 149.

11. Stephen Verney, *Into the New Age* (Centerport, N.Y.: John M. Fontana Publishing, 1976), 91–92.

Chapter 13

1. Mark S.J. Link, *Take Off Your Shoes* (Chicago: Argus Communications, 1972), 20.
2. Ibid., 12.
3. Ibid., 42.
4. From *A Testament of Devotion* by Thomas R. Kelly, 29. Copyright © 1941 by Harper & Row Publishers, Inc. Renewed 1969 by Lois Lael Kelly Stabler. New introduction Copyright © 1992 by HarperCollins Publishers, Inc. Reprinted by permission of HarperCollins Publishers, Inc.
5. Ibid., 35.
6. Ibid., 36.
7. Henry T. Blackaby and Claude V. King, *Experiencing God* (Nashville: Broadman & Holman, 1994), 23.
8. Kelly, *A Testament of Devotion*, 38–39.
9. Blackaby and King, *Experiencing God*, 157.
10. Ibid., 165.

BIBLIOGRAPHY

Andrews, Robert. *The Concise Columbia Dictionary of Quotations*. New York: Columbia University Press, 1989.

Anthony, Metropolitan et al. *Courage to Pray*. Crestwood, N.Y.: St. Vladimir's Seminary Press, 1997.

Barrett, William. *Death of the Soul: From Descartes to the Computer*. Garden City, N.Y.: Anchor/Doubleday, 1986.

Bennett, William J. "America, What's Gone Wrong?" *Current Thoughts and Trends*, July 1994, Vol.10, No. 7, 24.

_____. "A Nation's Spiritual Decay," *Sower* (Spring 1994), 10.

Berg, Elizabeth. "What's Your Hurry?" *Reader's Digest*, September 1993, 19.

Berman, Phillip L. *Search for Meaning*. New York: Ballantine, 1990.

Blackaby, Henry T., and Claude V. King. *Experiencing God*. Nashville: Broadman & Holman, 1994.

Blanchard, John, comp. *More Gathered Gold: A Treasury of Quotations for Christians*. Hertfordshire, England: Evangelical, 1986.

Bly, Robert, trans. *Times Alone: Selected Poems of Antonio MacHado*. Middletown, Conn: Wesleyan University Press, 1983.

Bowles, Linda. "Battle Rages Over America's Soul," *Daily Oklahoman*, 10 August 1994.

Boyd, Jeffrey H. *Affirming the Soul: Remarkable Conversations Between Mental Health Professionals and an Ordained Minister*. Cheshire, Conn.: Soul Research Institute, 1994.

Brown, Colin, ed. *The New International Dictionary of New Testament Theology.* Grand Rapids, Mich.: Zondervan, 1975.

Burns, Elizabeth. *The Late Liz.* New York: Meredith, 1957.

Canfield, Jack, and Mark Victor Hansen. *A Second Helping of Chicken Soup for the Soul: 101 More Stories to Open the Heart and Rekindle the Spirit.* Deerfield Beach, Fla.: Health Communications, 1995.

Carver, Raymond. "Meditations on a Line from Saint Teresa." *No Heroics Please: Raymond Carver Uncollected Writings.* New York: Vantage, 1992.

The Cloud of Unknowing. New York: Penguin, 1977.

Coles, Robert. *The Spiritual Life of Children.* Houghton Mifflin, 1990.

Corbiere, Edouard. *The Slave Trader.* New York: Harry N. Abrams, 1992.

Cousineau, Phil. *Soul: An Archaeology.* San Francisco: Harper San Francisco, 1994.

Cousins, Norman. *The Celebration of Life: A Dialogue on Hope, Spirit, and the Immortality of the Soul.* New York: Bantam, 1991.

Doan, Eleanor. *Speakers Sourcebook II.* Grand Rapids, Mich.: Zondervan, 1968.

Eliade, Mircea. "The Immortality of the Soul" in *No Souvenirs.* Translated by Fred H. Johnson, Jr. New York: Harper & Row, 1977.

Farrell, Frank. *Tabletalk.* June 1992.

Feder, Don. *A Jewish Conservative Looks at Pagan America.* Lafayette, La.: Huntington House, 1993.

Ferguson, Sheila. *Soul Food.* New York: Grove Press, 1989.

Fitzgerald, F. Scott, and Edmund Wilson, eds. *The Crackup*. New York: New Directions in Publishing Corp., 1993.

Fox, Matthew. *Meditations with Meister Eckhart*. Santa Fe: Bear & Company, 1983.

French, R.M., trans. *The Way of a Pilgrim*. San Francisco: Harper San Francisco, 1991.

Friedrich, Gerhard, ed. *Theological Dictionary of the New Testament*. Grand Rapids, Mich.: Wm. B. Eerdmans, 1974.

Gallup, George. "A Nation in Recovery," *Emerging Trends* 16, no. 10, December 1994, 1–2.

Gordon, Arthur. "Six Minutes of Awe," *Guideposts*, January 1992, 13.

Guralnick, Peter. *Sweet Soul Music: Rhythm and Blues and the Southern Dream of Freedom*. New York: Little Brown & Company, 1999.

Hale, Sue. "Collective Soul on the Mend," *Sunday Oklahoman*, 30 April 1995.

Hammerschlag, Carl A. *The Theft of the Spirit: A Journey to Spiritual Healing with Native Americans*. New York: Simon & Schuster, 1993.

Harvey, Paul. "It's Time for Americans to Return to Their Homes." *Daily Oklahoman*, 28 March 1994.

Hawthorne, Gerald F., and Ralph P. Martin, eds. *Dictionary of Paul and His Letters*. Downers Grove, Ill.: Inter-Varsity, 1993.

Herbert, Bob. "A Reckless Journey," *Black Chronicle*, 5 January 1995, 1–5.

Jones, Timothy. "Penchant for the Paranormal," *Leadership* 16, no. 1 (Winter 1994).

Keen, Sam. *Fire in the Belly*. New York: Bantam/Double-day/Dell Publishers, 1992.

Kelly, Thomas R. *A Testament of Devotion*. San Francisco: Harper San Francisco (reprint edition 1996).

à Kempis, Thomas. *The Imitation of Christ*. Nashville: Thomas Nelson, 1979.

Lacayo, Richard. "Are Music and Movies Killing America's Soul?" *Time*, 12 June 1995, 24–30.

Landers, Ann. Column. *Sunday Oklahoman and Times*, 25 December 1993.

——————. "The Saturday Review Youthworker Update." November 1994.

Link, Mark, S.J. *He Is the Still Point of the Turning World*. Chicago: Argus Communications, 1971.

——————. *Take Off Your Shoes*. Chicago: Argus Communications, 1972.

Marcus, Greil. *Mystery Train*. New York: Dutton, a division of Penguin USA, 1990.

Mead, Frank S., ed. *The Encyclopedia of Religious Quotations*. Westwood, N.J.: Fleming H. Revell, 1965.

Meditations with Hildegard of Bingen. Versions by Gabriele Uhlein. Sante Fe: Bear & Company, 1982.

Merton, Thomas. *Contemplative Prayer*. New York: Image Books, 1971.

——————. *Thoughts in Solitude*. New York: Farrar, Straus, Giroux, 1998.

Morrison, James D., ed. *Masterpieces of Religious Verse*. New York: Harper and Bros., 1948.

Needleman, Jacob. *Lost Christianity*. New York: Element Books, 1993.

Noffke, Suzanne, O.P., trans. *Catherine of Siena: The Dialogue*. New York: Paulist Press, 1980.

Nouwen, Henri J.M. *The Way of the Heart.* New York: Seabury, 1981.

Paton, Alan. *Instrument of Thy Peace: The Prayers of St. Francis.* New York: Seabury, 1968.

Pentz, Croft M. *The Complete Book of Zingers.* Wheaton, Ill.: Tyndale House, 1990.

Pepper, Margaret, comp. *The Harper Religious and Inspirational Quotation Companion.* New York: Harper & Row, 1989.

Pope John XXIII. *Journal of a Soul.* New York: McGraw-Hill, 1965.

Quoist, Michael. *Prayers.* New York: Sheed & Ward, 1963.

Raines, Robert A. *Creative Brooding.* New York: Macmillan, 1966.

_____. *Soundings.* New York: Harper & Row, 1970.

Rainie, Harrison. "The Buried Sounds of Children Crying." *U.S. News & World Report,* 1 May 1995, 10.

Raspberry, William. "We Must Learn Why We Are Producing Such Violent People," *Dallas Morning News,* 23 August 1993, 13A.

Reflections on the Jesus Prayer. Denville, N.J.: Dimension, 1948.

Richards, Mary Caroline. *Centering.* Middletown, Conn.: Wesleyan University Press, 1962.

Roberts, Alexander, and James Donaldson, eds. *The Ante-Nicene Fathers: Translations of the Writings of the Fathers Down to A.D. 325.* Grand Rapids, Mich.: Wm. B. Eerdmans, 1989.

Rosenthal, Marvin J. "America's Meteoric Descent into Darkness," *Pulpit Helps,* August 1994, 24.

Saint Teresa of Avila. *The Interior Castle.* Translated and edited by E. Allison Peers. New York: Image, 1961.

Sardello, Robert. "Facing the World with Soul," in *Facing the World with Soul.* Hudson, N.Y.: Lindisfarne, 1991.

Schaff, Philip, ed. *A Select Library of the Nicene and Post-Nicene Fathers of the Christian Church.* Grand Rapids, Mich.: Wm. B. Eerdmans, 1989.

Sheen, Fulton J. *Life of Christ.* New York: McGraw-Hill Co., Inc., 1958.

Simpson, James B., comp. *Simpson's Contemporary Quotations.* Boston: Houghton Mifflin, 1988.

Simsic, Wayne. *Praying with John of the Cross.* Winona, Minn.: Christian Brothers, 1993.

Singer, June. *Boundaries of the Soul: The Practice of Jung's Psychology.* Garden City, N.Y.: Doubleday, 1972.

Steiner, Rudolf. "The Two Streams of the Soul." *Metamorphoses of the Soul,* vol. 2. Translated by C. Davy and C. mon Arnim. Anthroposophic Press, 1990.

Styron, William. *Sophie's Choice.* New York: Bantam Books, 1979.

Swindoll, Charles. *Stress Fractures.* Grand Rapids, Mich.: Zondervan, 1990.

ten Boom, Corrie. *The Hiding Place.* Washington Depot, Conn.: Chosen Books, 1971.

Thompson, Francis. "The Hound of Heaven." *Masterpieces of Religious Verse.* New York: Harper & Brothers, 1948.

dd, Loretto. *Tortoise the Trickster and Other Folktales from Cameroon.* Philadelphia: Benjamins North American, 1982.

Rhonda Thomas, comp. *The International The-is of Quotations.* New York: Harper & Row, 1970.

Underhill, Evelyn. *Mysticism.* Cleveland and New York: World Publishing, 1970.

Underwood, John. *The Boston Globe.*

Verney, Stephen. *Into the New Age.* Centerport, N.Y.: John M. Fontana Publishing, 1976.

Walker, Alice. "They Want Your Soul." *Living by the Word: Selected Writings: 1973–1987.* New York: Harcourt, Brace & Company, 1988.

Walsh, Kenneth T. "The Soul and Character of America." *U.S News & World Report,* 8 May 1995, 10.

Ward, Benedicta, trans. *The Sayings of the Desert Fathers.* London: Mowbrays, 1975.

Watson, David. *Discipleship.* Hodder & Stoughton, 1981.

Wells, Jr., Albert M., comp. *Inspiring Quotations: Contemporary and Classical.* Nashville: Thomas Nelson, 1988.

Wiesel, Elie. *Night.* New York: Bantam, 1960.

Wright, Robert. "The Evolution of Despair." *Time,* 28 August 1995, 50.